*The Crisp Appro[ach]*

# money management using

# LOTUS 1-2-3

## by William Barth

The *Crisp Computer* Series

Editor: Toni Murray
Project Manager: Jane Granoff
Interior Design: Kathleen Gadway
Cover Design: Kathleen Gadway

Library of Congress No 94-070484

ISBN 1-56052-276-3

Lotus and 1-2-3 are registered trademarks of Lotus Development Corporation.

# Crisp Computer Book Series

These books are not like other books. Inspired by the widely successful "Fifty-Minute" Crisp Books, these books provide the least you need to know in order to use today's most popular application software packages. Specifically designed for either self-study or business training, they are "the fifty-minute books that teach!"

These guides are not for technical wizards or power users. They are for the average business person who is not familiar with computers nor comfortable with a particular software package—such as WordPerfect, Lotus 1-2-3, or Excel.

In most everyday computer applications, employees, managers, and students do not need to learn every feature and capability of their software. What most business users want is simply the amount of knowledge—delivered as quickly and painlessly as possible—to perform specific duties: write the letter, report or newsletter; create the budget or sales forecast; set up a mailing list; and other important business tasks. These books use everyday business examples to guide readers step-by-step through just those commands that they will use most.

Concise and practical, the Crisp fifty-minute computer books provide quick, easy ways to learn today's most popular computer software applications.

# Other Books in the Crisp Computer Series

# Table of Contents

# Introduction

The electronic spreadsheet program has been described as one of the most revolutionary programs ever written for the micro-computer. It was the first program that made it possible for microcomputer users without programming expertise to develop applications. The Lotus 1-2-3 program is one of the best-selling spreadsheet programs. It has been around since the development of the IBM Personal Computer.

Electronic spreadsheets allow you to enter data, do math calculations with the data, sort the data, draw graphs based on the data, store the data on disk, and print reports based on the data. An electronic spreadsheet program is ideal for generating budgets, financial statements, stock portfolio analyses, and inventory lists. Nearly any task that involves keeping data in rows and columns can be performed more efficiently with an electronic spreadsheet than with a pad of ruled paper. When you modify one data item, the spreadsheet program automatically recalculates all formulas the change affects. This allows you to try different variables for different scenarios. In other words, the program allows you to ask "What if" questions. You can, for example, ask "What if the interest rate were 9.5%?" A few keystrokes, and Lotus 1-2-3 tells you the answer. Then you can ask "What if the interest rate were 10%?" Again, in seconds, the spreadsheet program tells you the answer. The use of an electronic spreadsheet replaces hours spent using paper, pencil, and erasers.

This text is designed for people unfamiliar with Lotus 1-2-3. Although this book was written to accompany DOS versions of the program, all examples and commands in the text will work with Lotus 1-2-3 for Windows if you use the Lotus Classic menu available in the Windows version.

The examples in this text focus on practical documents and financial statements—the kind you are likely to use if you work in a small business and deal with accountants, suppliers, customers, or creditors. For example, in Lesson 3 you will learn how to prepare a budget with Lotus; in Lesson 4 you create a worksheet to determine loan payments. Lessons 5 and 6 cover the fundamentals of setting up a Balance Sheet and an Income Statement. In addition, the appendices provide such useful reference material as a summary of common worksheet tasks (Appendix B) and a sampling of the most commonly used accounting documents and templates (Appendix C).

## How to Use This Book

The lessons in this book take you through, step-by-step, a sequence of building financial worksheets. The lessons begin with a simple worksheet that keeps track of expenses. Succeeding lessons present more complicated worksheets. Each lesson introduces new Lotus 1-2-3 concepts, building on concepts learned in prior lessons. Do each lesson in sequence. If you are familiar with computer hardware and have used a spreadsheet before, you may be able to start with Lesson 2. Lesson 2 is the longest lesson because it introduces the basics of using Lotus.

As you progress through the lessons, you will learn how to enter data, modify data, enter formulas, sort data, draw graphs, save worksheets to disk, retrieve saved files, and print worksheets.

## Conventions Used in This Book

This book uses visual clues and graphic shorthand to help you work quickly and effectively.

**Examples**

**References to named keys on the keyboard (such as Esc, Home, and Alt) appear in a font designed to look like the tops of the keys themselves. (This form is called keycaps.)**

Home

**Key names separated by a hyphen (-) indicate that you must press and hold down the first key while you press the second key.**

Alt-F3

**Key names separated by a comma indicate that you must press the first key, release it, then press the second key and release it.**

End, Home

**Words in bold print are important terms. Definitions of these terms appear in the glossary.**

A **cell** is a ...

Something that you must type appears in a contrasting typeface.

Type: TOTAL

Menu choices separated by a comma indicate that you must make the first choice cited, then the second, then the third, and so on.

Print,
Printer,
Align, Go
Page, Quit

# 1

## OBJECTIVES

- Distinguish hardware from software
- Start up Lotus 1-2-3
- Identify parts of the Lotus 1-2-3 screen
- Move from one part of the worksheet to another
- Use the menu
- Quit Lotus 1-2-3

# Getting Started

## Learning About Computer Hardware

The **hardware** of your computer system is the equipment that forms it. Computer hardware consists of five main parts:

**Input devices.** An **input device** is used to enter data and the directions for processing it. Examples of input devices include a keyboard, a mouse, and a scanner.

**Internal memory.** Also called **random-access memory (RAM)**, **internal memory** holds the program and data you are currently using. Prior to running a program, you must load it into internal memory. Internal memory is referred to as volatile. This means that the contents of internal memory will be lost if the power is turned off. Because internal memory is volatile, you should save your work frequently.

**External memory.** The most common kind of external memory is a disk. **External memory** uses a technology different than that used by internal memory; as a result, external memory can retain its contents even after the electricity is turned off. External memory acts like a library, holding copies of all the programs and data you may want to use. However, to actually use the data or a program, it must be loaded into internal memory.

**Microprocessor.** The **microprocessor** is the "brain" of the system. It analyzes each instruction in the program and sends signals to the other parts of the computer, directing the execution of the instruction. Additionally, the microprocessor does the math calculations required by the program.

**Output devices.** An **output device** displays or prints on-screen instructions, data that has been input, or the results of processing. Typically, a computer system has a display screen and printer as output devices.

Of the devices cited in the previous list, the one you need to become most familiar with is the keyboard.

## The Keyboard

To be productive with Lotus 1-2-3, you must be familiar with the frequently used keys on the keyboard. Find each of the following keys on your keyboard:

| | |
|---|---|
| Esc | Resets the Lotus 1-2-3 system and returns it to the ready state. Usually, this key is in the top left corner of the keyboard. |
| / | Causes the menu to appear at the top of the screen, temporarily replacing what was shown there. (The action of appearing in this way is called popping up.) This key is usually in the lower-right section of the part of the computer keyboard that looks like a typewriter keyboard. Typically, / is above the right corner of the space bar. |
| Pg Up | Moves the cell pointer up one full screen. The **cell pointer** is a rectangle that contrasts with the background color of the screen. By moving the rectangle, you can access different cells of the worksheet. |

| | |
|---|---|
| Pg Dn | Moves the cell pointer down one full screen. |
| Home | Returns the cell pointer to the upper-left corner of the worksheet, the primary work area of Lotus 1-2-3. This key is usually to the right of the "typewriter" keyboard. |
| Caps Lock | Enables you to type uppercase letters, without holding down Shift. |
| Enter | Allows you to signal that an operation is complete. Located to the right of the home row (the second row from the top of the typewriter keyboard). |

In addition, you should know the location of the function keys. These keys are usually in a row at the top of the computer keyboard. Each function key is labeled with a number, and each number is preceded by the letter *F*. The **function keys** allow you to implement, in one keystroke, instructions that take the computer several steps to complete. In this sense, function keys represent shortcuts.

# Learning About Computer Software

In addition to hardware, you will need software. **Software** refers to programs, which are the instructions that tell the hardware what to do. For the purposes of this book, the software is Lotus 1-2-3.

# Starting Up Lotus 1-2-3

The start-up procedure for Lotus 1-2-3 varies according to whether your computer has two floppy-disk drives or one floppy-disk drive and one hard-disk drive. To begin the start-up procedure, boot the computer, loading DOS. The prompt (A:\> or C:\>) should appear. Then follow the instructions in one of the two sections that follow, whichever is appropriate for your computer.

## Using Dual Floppy-Disk Drives

If you are using a system without a hard disk, you must load Lotus 1-2-3 from a floppy disk. Insert the Lotus 1-2-3 System Disk into drive A. Insert a data disk in drive B.

**Type:**     **123**

**Press:**     [Enter]

If you are using a version in the Lotus 1-2-3 release 2 series, with a floppy disk system or a hard disk system, you must type **LOTUS** (instead of 123) when starting up the program. This will enable you to print graphs. When the introductory screen displays and the 1-2-3 menu item is highlighted at the top of the screen, you must press [Enter] to proceed into the Lotus 1-2-3 program.

## Using a Hard Disk Drive

If your DOS prompt is C:\>, you need to change the directory to the one that contains Lotus 1-2-3. This directory is normally named 123.

**Type:**     **CD 123**

When the DOS prompt is C:\123> (or a variation of this):

**Type:**     **123**

**Press:**     [Enter]

The display you now have on your screen is a blank worksheet. A **worksheet** is a grid of rows and columns in which you store data and formulas. *Figure 1.1* presents a Lotus 1-2-3 worksheet. The worksheet is just one part of the screen.

*Figure 1.1*

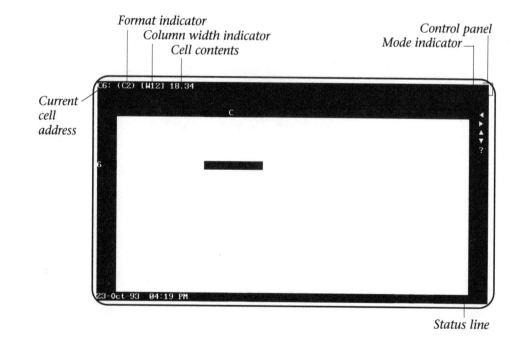

Format indicator
Column width indicator
Cell contents
Control panel
Mode indicator
Current cell address
Status line

# Learning About the Spreadsheet Screen

As you know, the worksheet is a grid of rows and columns. The rows are numbered; the columns have letters as headings. The area where a column and a row intersect is called a **cell.**

Twenty rows are visible on the screen at one time. The entire worksheet consists of 256 columns and 8,192 rows. Column headings are the letters A to IV. The portion of the worksheet that is visible at any one time is called the **window**. The window is moved by using keys such as [Tab], [Pg Up], and [Pg Dn]. Moving the window is called scrolling.

Try scrolling.

**Press:**         [Pg Dn] **(several times)**

**Press:**         [Home] **(to return to cell A1)**

The worksheet takes up most of the room on the screen. But the screen consists of two other elements: the control panel and the status line.

The top three rows of the screen are the **control panel**. The control panel displays information about the following:

**Current cell address.**   The position of the cell pointer determines the current cell address. For example, if the cell pointer is in Column C, row 6, the current cell address is C6.

**Format.**   The **format** is the manner in which numbers are displayed. In Currency format, for example, numbers appear with dollar signs in front of them. In *Figure 1.1*, the format indicator C2 means that the numbers in the worksheet are displayed in Currency format, with a decimal point, and with two digits to the right of the decimal point.

**Column width.**   All cells in a worksheet start out with a width of 9 characters. The width of 9 remains the **default**, the value assumed by Lotus 1-2-3 at startup, unless you change it. After you change it, the control panel displays the new value. In *Figure 1.1,* W12 indicates that the current column width is 12.

**Cell contents.** Before you finalize the data that will appear in a cell, the data (the cell contents) is displayed in the control panel.

**Mode.** The mode is the status of the program. The mode indicator, which appears in the control panel, is a word that appears in uppercase letters: READY, WAIT, and ERROR, for example.

In addition to the indicators mentioned in the preceding list and shown in Figure 1.1, the control panel sometimes displays a menu. The first Lotus 1-2-3 menu pops up after you press ⃞/⃞. At that point, the indicators disappear. Try calling up the menu.

**Press:**        ⃞/⃞

See how the menu is displayed in the control panel? Notice that the mode indicator has changed to MENU. To set the indicator back to READY:

**Press:**        ⃞Esc⃞

At the bottom of the screen display is the **status line**. The status line contains information about the date, time, and the setting of ⃞Caps Lock⃞, ⃞Num Lock⃞, and the like.

## Moving Around in a Worksheet

This portion of the lesson will give you a chance to practice moving the cell pointer from cell to cell. You will use several different keys.

**Press:**        ⃞Home⃞ **(to be sure you are at cell A1)**

**Press:**        ⃞↓⃞ **(three times)**

Note that the control panel reports that the current cell address is A4. To move the cell pointer to cell D4:

**Press:**        ⃞→⃞ **(three times)**

**Press:**        ⃞Pg Dn⃞

Note that the cell pointer has moved down 20 rows from its previous position. As you recall, ⃞Pg Dn⃞ scrolls the window down. ⃞Pg Up⃞ scrolls the window up.

**Press:** [End]

**Press:** [↓]

The cell pointer is in row 8,192. If the worksheet was full of data, the cell pointer would be in the last row of data.

**Press:** [Home] **(to return to cell A1)**

**Press:** [Tab] **(three times)**

As you see, pressing [Tab] scrolls the window to the right. Note how the columns after column Z are labeled AA, AB, AC, and so on.

**Press:** [End]

**Press:** [→]

The cell pointer is now at the right edge of the worksheet, column IV.

**Press:** [Shift]-[Tab]

The window scrolls to the left.

**Press:** [Home] **(to return to cell A1)**

Another way to go to a specific cell is to use F5.

**Press:** [F5]

Note that a message has appeared in the control panel; the message asks what address you want to go to.

**Type:** **D6**

**Press:** [Enter]

The list that follows reviews the keys you just used and cites several others.

[Home]     Returns the cell pointer to cell A1.

[↑][↓][→][←]     Moves the cell pointer one cell, in the direction indicated by the arrow.

[Pg Up]     Moves the window up 20 rows.

| | |
|---|---|
| Pg Dn | Moves the window down 20 rows. |
| Tab | Scrolls the window right. |
| Shift-Tab | Scrolls the window left. |
| End | Moves the cell pointer up to the cell preceding a blank cell, a fast way to get to the top of a column of data. Use End with the other arrow keys to move similarly, in the direction indicated by the arrow. |
| F5 | Displays a message in the control panel, asking you for the address you want to go to. You simply type the cell address and press Enter. |

## Using the Menu System

The Lotus 1-2-3 menu system provides access to the commands that let you do things with a worksheet—things like printing, saving, widening its columns, and the like. Pressing / causes the menu to appear in the control panel.

As *Figure 1.2* shows, the menu appears on two lines of the control panel. The first line of the menu contains the menu choices. The second line contains an explanation of what will happen if you choose the highlighted item. The highlighted item is the one that appears in a rectangle that contrasts with its background. If choosing a highlighted menu item will call a submenu, the second line

The keyboard includes two similar keys: a slash / and backslash \. Be sure to use the appropriate key. Pressing / causes the menu to appear in the control panel.

*Figure 1.2*

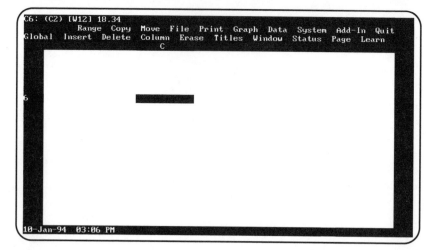

contains the submenu choices you will get by picking the high-lighted item. By pressing ⬅ or ➡, you can move the highlight to a different item.

Try it:

**Press:** ⌿

The menu appears in the control panel and the mode indicator changes to MENU.

**Press:** ➡ **(twice)**

The highlight now rests on the third menu option, Copy. See how the line under the menu choices changes as you highlight different menu items? When you have placed the highlight on the desired menu choice, you would press Enter to select the high-lighted item. If you changed your mind, you would press Esc to cancel the menu selection. For now, move the highlight back to Worksheet.

**Press:** Enter

A submenu appears. Try moving the highlight to Column.

**Press:** Enter

Now the screen displays a new menu. You don't have to use this menu right now, so cancel the selection:

**Press:** Esc

You have moved back one level in the submenu hierarchy. To get out of the menu and return the mode indicator to READY:

**Press:** Esc **(twice)**

To work efficiently with Lotus 1-2-3, remember these instructions:

- To call up the menu, press ⌿.

- Choose a menu option by placing the highlight on it and press-ing Enter.

- To return the mode indicator to READY and cancel a menu, press Esc.

- After you call a specific menu, you can use a shortcut for choosing a menu item: Simply type the first letter of the name of the item. You do not have to press Enter after typing the letter.

# Quitting Lotus 1-2-3

If you use the shortcut method for picking a menu item, do *not* press Enter after typing the first letter of the name of your menu choice. Press the letter only.

When you finish using Lotus 1-2-3, you must call up the menu to tell the program you want to quit. To call up the menu:

**Press:** /

Now either:

**Type:** Q (the letter Q stands for *Quit.*)

*or* move the highlight to Quit in the menu and then:

**Press:** Enter

The system will now ask you if you are sure you want to quit Lotus 1-2-3. You either:

**Type:** Y (the letter Y stands for *Yes.*)

*or* move the highlight to Yes in the menu and then:

**Press:** Enter

The DOS prompt appears. You are ready to load another program or turn your computer off.

# 2
## LESSON

### OBJECTIVES

- Record expenses on a worksheet
- Correct data entry errors
- Erase a worksheet
- Use @SUM and simple formulas
- Modify column width
- Format numbers
- Save and retrieve disk files
- Print a worksheet

# Creating a Travel Expense Summary

Many people have to travel on overnight business trips. A spreadsheet program provides an excellent way of keeping track of expenses for these trips. The data accumulated in the worksheet can be used to project the future travel costs. In addition, the worksheet can provide data when it comes time to prepare an income statement.

If you haven't already loaded Lotus 1-2-3 into your computer, do so now; a blank worksheet should appear on the screen. You are now ready to learn the basics of entering data into a worksheet.

A worksheet cell can hold three different types of data: labels, numbers, and formulas. Each is entered in a specific way.

# Entering Labels

A **label** is descriptive text entered into a cell. A label can be a phrase, word, or character. It can incorporate numbers that are not used in calculations, and punctuation. A label can be:

**Alphabetic.**  Column headings are examples of alphabetic data.

**Numeric.**  Phone numbers, social security numbers, and zip codes are examples of numeric data.

**Numeric data is not used for math calculations.**

Labels always start with a code called a **label prefix**. Lotus 1-2-3 uses the label prefix to determine how the label should be displayed in the column: left-aligned, centered, or right-aligned. The prefixes allow you to choose the alignment that looks or works best. If you fail to start the label with a label prefix, Lotus 1-2-3 automatically defaults to left alignment.

The three label prefix characters are:

| | | |
|---|---|---|
| ′ (apostrophe) | The default, left-aligns the label |
| ^ (caret) | Centers the label |
| " (quotation mark) | Right-aligns the label |

In regard to correcting mistakes in label data: If you discover the mistake before pressing (Enter), use (Backspace) and retype. If you discover it after pressing (Enter), retype and press (Enter) again.

As you practice working with labels, you may well make a mistake or two. If you make a mistake and realize it before you press (Enter), use (Backspace) to erase characters up to the mistake, then type the correct data. If you discover a mistake after pressing (Enter), simply retype the data and press (Enter) again. Lotus 1-2-3 will replace the incorrect cell contents with the new data.

Now try entering data. In cell A1:

**Type:**     JULY

**Press:**     (Enter)

The word is left-aligned within the cell. Look at the control panel in the top left corner of the screen. Notice how it indicates that cell A1 contains ′JULY. The label prefix character is there, but it does not appear in the cell. It provides Lotus 1-2-3 with instructions about alignment.

Move the cell pointer to cell A2.

**Type:** ^JULY (The caret is usually on the "Shift" of the 6 key, at the top of the typewriter keyboard.)

**Press:** [Enter]

Notice how the word is centered in the cell. Again, you see that the control panel contains ^JULY but the cell displays JULY.

Move the cell pointer to cell A3.

**Type:** "JULY

**Press:** [Enter]

The word JULY is right-aligned in the cell. Since numbers automatically right-align, column headings should usually right-align too, so they are directly over the numbers.

Move the cell pointer to cell A4.

**Type:** 12

**Press:** [Enter]

Don't you think the heading JULY looks better right-aligned?

*Figure 2.1* shows how the labels you have added so far should look. In addition, it shows how the screen will look after you finish adding numbers according to instructions in the next section.

# Entering Numbers

A number is easy to enter. You simply type 12. Lotus 1-2-3 calls numbers values. When you are entering numbers, the mode indicator displays the word VALUE. For practice, in cell A5:

**Type:** 22

In cell A6:

**Type:** 31

*Figure 2.1*

# Entering Formulas

A **formula** tells Lotus 1-2-3 to calculate the contents of a cell by using data from other cells. Formulas normally begin with a plus sign or a left parenthesis. **Arithmetic operators** tell Lotus 1-2-3 what math operations to do with the data in the formula. The arithmetic operators this book discusses are:

| Symbol | Means |
|--------|----------|
| + | Add |
| – | Subtract |
| * | Multiply |
| / | Divide |

You could use a formula to total a column of numbers, for example. Move the cell pointer to cell A7.

**Type:**     **+A4+A5+A6**

**Press:**     ⌷Enter⌸

If you look in the control panel, it displays the formula you typed; if you look at cell A7, it displays the sum, 65. If you change any of the numbers used by a formula, Lotus 1-2-3 automatically recalculates the formula. To verify this, move the cell pointer to cell A6.

**Type:**        25

**Press:**        Enter

See how the value in cell A7 has changed to 59?

# Correcting Data

Eventually, no matter how good a typist you are, you will make a keying error. As you have read, there are several different ways to fix an error, depending on whether you discover the error before or after you press Enter. This section will review what you already know about correcting typographical errors and provide a few more options for error correction.

You have seen that, as you type data, it is displayed on the second line in the control panel. If you discover the error by glancing at the control panel prior to pressing Enter, use Backspace deleting one character at a time, until the cursor backs up to the error and removes it. Then type the correct data. Try it. Move the cell pointer to cell C11.

**Type:**        APREL

but don't press Enter. To correct the data:

**Press:**        Backspace **(twice, until it removes EL)**

**Type:**        IL

**Press:**        Enter **(to complete data entry)**

If the mode indicator is the word READY, you cannot use Backspace to fix the data. One option is to retype the data and press Enter. Move the cell pointer to cell C12.

**Type:**        APREL

but don't press Enter yet. Look at the mode indicator. It is LABEL.

**Press:**  Enter

The data is entered into the cell and the mode indicator has changed from LABEL to READY. To correct the error:

**Type:**  APRIL

**Press:**  Enter

The correct data has been entered into the cell, overwriting the previous data.

Another way to correct data if you have already pressed Enter is to use F2. This key is called the Edit key. It is used to edit data from the READY mode. Move the cell pointer to cell C13.

**Type:**  AVREL

**Press:**  Enter

**Press:**  F2 **(to change the mode indicator from READY to EDIT)**

Now you can use the left and right arrow keys to move to the incorrect character and delete it.

There are two keys you can use in the EDIT mode to remove characters: Backspace erases the character to the left of the cursor; Del erases the character the cursor is on. Looking at the left side of the second line in the control panel, move the cursor to the R.

**Press:**  Backspace **(to remove the V)**

**Type:**  P **(to insert it into the text)**

Now remove a character by using Del. Move the cursor to the E.

**Press:**  Del

**Type:**  I

**Press:**  Enter

# Erasing a Worksheet from Internal Memory

The worksheet on your screen is currently in internal memory. It has not been saved to disk. (You will learn how to save files to disk later in this lesson.) You no longer need this worksheet, so you can ask Lotus 1-2-3 to erase it.

**Press:**    / (to call up the menu, in the control panel)

You will select a menu choice by moving the highlight right or left, to the desired choice.

**Select:**    **Worksheet**

**Press:**    Enter

A new menu appears.

**Select:**    **Erase**

**Press:**    Enter

Lotus 1-2-3 now asks if you really want to erase the worksheet.

**Select:**    **Yes**

**Press:**    Enter

When you try to erase a worksheet that hasn't been saved yet, Lotus 1-2-3 will protect you from losing it forever by asking if you want to erase the file even though it hasn't been saved.

**Select:**    **Yes**

**Press:**    Enter

Remember that there are two methods of picking an item from a menu after you have pressed /. One way is to move the highlight to the desired item and press Enter. A shortcut is to type the first letter of the menu selection. If you use the second method, do *not* press Enter.

# Preparing a Travel Expense Summary

You now have a blank worksheet and are ready to prepare a travel expense summary.

Type the following headings in the cells indicated, including a label prefix where shown:

| | |
|---|---|
| A1 | **TRAVEL EXPENSE RECORD** |
| A5 | **DATE** |
| B5 | **DEST.** |
| C5 | **EXPLANATION** |
| D5 | **"TRAVEL** |
| E5 | **"HOTEL** |
| F5 | **"MEALS** |
| G5 | **"TOTAL** |

## Changing Column Width

When you typed the data in cell A1, it overflowed from A1 into B1 and C1. You won't use B1 or C1, so it is acceptable for the label to overflow. Now look at cell C5. It isn't wide enough to display the entire word EXPLANATION. Unlike the label in A1, however, the label in cell C5 can't overflow into D5; data will appear in D5. You need to widen column C from the default column width of 9 to a larger size. You are going to change the column width to 14 so the cell is long enough to hold explanations. Move the cell pointer to any cell in column C. Observe the control panel as you do the following:

| | |
|---|---|
| Press: | $\boxed{/}$ (to call up the menu) |
| Select: | **Worksheet** |
| Select: | **Column** |
| Select: | **Set-Width** |
| Type: | **14** |

*Figure 2.2*

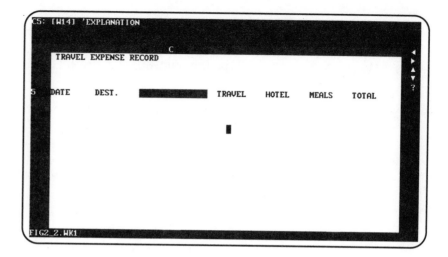

**Press:**     Enter

Your worksheet should now look like *Figure 2.2*.

Move the cell pointer to cell A7

**Type:**     3/12/94 (A date)

**Press:**     Enter

Look at cell A7. It contains 0.002659. The reason is that Lotus 1-2-3 interpreted 3/12/94 as a formula. It divided 3 by 12 and then divided the answer by 94, giving 0.002659. You need to tell Lotus 1-2-3 to interpret this as a label, not a formula. With the cell pointer still in cell A7

**Press:**     F2

Move the cursor to the leftmost character (the 3) and add a label prefix.

**Type:**     ' (apostrophe)

**Press:**     Enter

The label now appears as it should, as a date. Whenever you want to enter data that contains slashes or dashes (such as dates, social security numbers, or phone numbers), precede the data with a label prefix. This will prevent Lotus 1-2-3 from treating the label as a formula.

Type the following data in the cell indicated:

| | |
|---|---|
| B7 | **CHICAGO** |
| C7 | **TRADE CONV.** |
| D7 | **318** |
| E7 | **270** |
| F7 | **225** |

Now you need to type a formula in cell G7 to total the expenses for the trip. You actually have two choices for the formula. You can type +D7+E7+F7 or you can use a shorthand method to implement a formula. The shorthand method is called a function. A **function** is a predefined formula. Into it you enter the range of data to be used. A **range** is a block of cells. In a function, you define a range by typing the address of the upper-left cell, a period, and the address of the lower-right cell. The range A6.C10 includes all cells from A6 to A10, B6 to B10, and C6 to C10. Many Lotus 1-2-3 commands use ranges, so it is important to understand them.

Functions start with the @ symbol followed by a word describing the function. The function you are going to use for practice is @SUM. The **@SUM function** needs to know what cells you want to sum and then it tells Lotus 1-2-3 to calculate the total you have asked for. To add cells D7, E7, and F7, you write the function @SUM(D7.F7). Move the cell pointer to cell G7.

**Type:**       @**SUM(D7.F7)**

**Press:**      [Enter]

Cell G7 should display the answer, 813.

Note that, after a function is entered into a cell, Lotus 1-2-3 displays the function in the control panel with *two* periods separating the range cells.

Type the following data in the cells indicated. (Where a label prefix is included, be sure to type it.)

| | |
|---|---|
| C8 | '3 NIGHTS |
| A10 | '4/12/94 |
| B10 | DETROIT |
| C10 | FORD PRESENT. |
| D10 | 595 |
| E10 | 123 |
| F10 | 86 |
| C11 | OVERNIGHT |
| A13 | '6/22/94 |
| B13 | NEW YORK |
| C13 | BUYING TRIP |
| D13 | 223 |
| E13 | 255 |
| F13 | 330 |
| C14 | '4 NIGHTS |
| C17 | ANNUAL TOTALS |
| D17 | @SUM(D7.D13) |

Your worksheet should look like *Figure 2.3*.

## Copying Cell Contents

You need to total values in several places on the worksheet. However, instead of actually typing the formulas, you are going to copy them from other cells. Lotus 1-2-3 will modify the @SUM function so it uses the appropriate data. Move the highlight to cell D17. Look at @SUM function displayed in the left side of the control panel. It instructs Lotus 1-2-3 to add up the numbers in

*Figure 2.3*

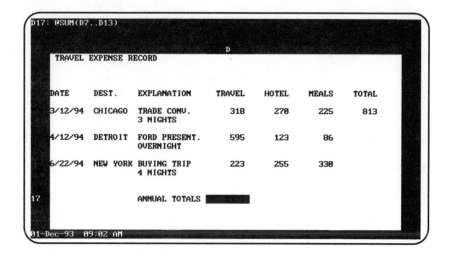

```
D17: @SUM(D7..D13)

                                               D
    TRAVEL EXPENSE RECORD


    DATE      DEST.    EXPLANATION     TRAVEL   HOTEL   MEALS   TOTAL
    3/12/94   CHICAGO  TRADE CONV.       318     270     225     813
                       3 NIGHTS

    4/12/94   DETROIT  FORD PRESENT.     595     123      86
                       OVERNIGHT

    6/22/94   NEW YORK BUYING TRIP       223     255     330
                       4 NIGHTS

17                     ANNUAL TOTALS  ████████

01-Dec-93  09:02 AM
```

column D, the seven cells from D7 to D13. If you copy that formula to another column, Lotus 1-2-3 will adjust the formula to add the seven cells in that column.

Make sure the cell pointer is on cell D17. Observe the control panel as you do the following:

**Press:**  ⁄

**Select:**  **C**opy (from the menu)

Look at the control panel. It is asking you if you want to copy from cell D17. You do, so

**Press:**  Enter

Now the control panel is asking you where the copy of the formula should go.

**Type:**  **E17.G17 (to total the values in columns E, F, and G, respectively)**

**Press:**  Enter

Also, you need a total in column G for rows 10 and 13. Move the cell pointer to cell G7.

**Press:**  ⁄

| | |
|---|---|
| Select: | **C**opy (from the menu) |
| Press: | [Enter] (to copy the function from G7) |
| Type: | **G10** (the destination) |
| Press: | [Enter] |
| Press: | [/] |
| Select: | **C**opy |
| Press: | [Enter] |
| Type: | **G13** |
| Press: | [Enter] |

When you copied the function from D17 to E17, F17, and G17, the cells receiving the function were adjacent, so you could copy it in one operation. The totals in column G have blank rows between them, so you had to copy each function individually. Your worksheet should look like *Figure 2.4*.

## Moving Data in the Worksheet

Lotus 1-2-3 also provides the ability to move data from one cell to another. The steps for moving are similar to those for copying. The difference in the result is that Copy reproduces the data in

*Figure 2.4*

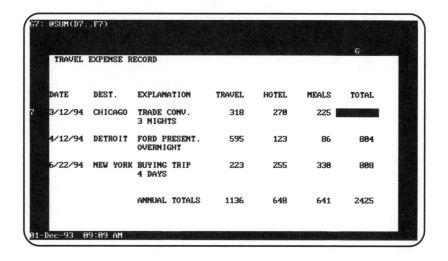

the new location, leaving the data intact in the original location, but Move erases the data at the original location and places it in the new location. To move data, you would press ⌷ and select Move. Then you would type the current cell address of the data, press Enter, indicate the new address, and press Enter.

## Formatting Numbers

As you know, the term *format*, in Lotus 1-2-3 refers to the punctuation and number of decimal places that appear. You are going to format the numbers in the range D7 through G17 with dollar signs and two decimal places, the basic Currency format. Observe the control panel as you do the following:

**Press:**     ⌷

**Select:**    **Range**

**Select:**    **Format**

**Select:**    **Currency**

Since you want two decimal places, the Lotus 1-2-3 default,

**Press:**    Enter

If you didn't want two decimal places, you could type the number desired.

**Type:**    **D7.G17 (the range)**

**Press:**    Enter

Your worksheet should look like *Figure 2.5.*

Notice that asterisks appear in several cells. This indicates that the cell is not big enough to hold the formatted numbers. You will widen the cells in columns D through G. The new width will be 10. Look at the menus in the control panel as you do the following:

**Press:**    ⌷

**Select:**    **Worksheet, Column, Column-Range, Set-Width**

**Type:**    **D1.G1 (to indicate the columns to be resized)**

*Figure 2.5*

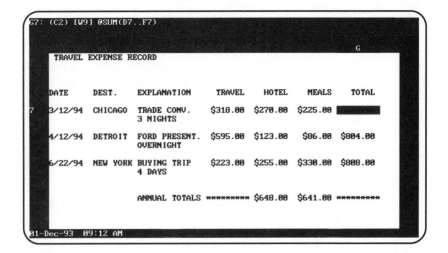

G7: (C2) [W9] @SUM(D7..F7)

TRAVEL EXPENSE RECORD

| DATE | DEST. | EXPLANATION | TRAVEL | HOTEL | MEALS | TOTAL |
|------|-------|-------------|--------|-------|-------|-------|
| 7 3/12/94 | CHICAGO | TRADE CONV. 3 NIGHTS | $318.00 | $270.00 | $225.00 | ▓▓▓▓▓ |
| 4/12/94 | DETROIT | FORD PRESENT. OVERNIGHT | $595.00 | $123.00 | $86.00 | $804.00 |
| 6/22/94 | NEW YORK | BUYING TRIP 4 DAYS | $223.00 | $255.00 | $330.00 | $808.00 |
| | | ANNUAL TOTALS | ********* | $648.00 | $641.00 | ********* |

01-Dec-93   09:12 AM

**Press:** [Enter]

**Type:** 10 (to indicate the new width)

**Press:** [Enter]

Now the columns with numbers are big enough to hold the data. In this instance you set a range of columns, so you used the menu items

Worksheet, Column, Column-Range, Set-Width

If you were changing just one column, you would use the menu items

Worksheet, Column, Set-Width

# Saving the Work to Disk

Lotus 1-2-3 will save the worksheet to the default disk drive, the disk drive Lotus 1-2-3 assumes you want to use in the absence of specific instruction to the contrary. To check the default drive:

**Press:** [/]

**Select:** **F**ile, **D**irectory

If the prompt is C:\, you are going to be saving to the hard disk. If the prompt contains B: or A:, you will save to a diskette in drive A or B. If the current setting is not where you want it to be, type the correct path. The path indicates the disk drive and directory Lotus 1-2-3 should use for disk operations. When the path is correct:

**Press:** [Enter]

To actually save the file to disk, you will use the File, Save menu choices. Lotus will ask you for a disk file name. You must follow rules in assigning names. No more than eight characters can be in a name. You can use only letters, numbers, and the underscore ( _ ). The name must be one word, with no embedded spaces. JAN BUDG would be an invalid name because it contains an embedded space. You could correct the name by calling the file JAN_BUDG or JANBUDG. Now you will save the file. Look at the control panel while doing the following:

**Press:** [/]

**Select:** **File, Save**

**Type:** **TRAVEL (the file name)**

**Press:** [Enter]

To see what is saved on the disk:

**Press:** [/]

**Select:** **File, List, Worksheet**

If you don't see the file name TRAVEL in the list of saved files, press [Enter] and repeat the steps for saving a file. After looking at the list of saved files, press [Enter] to continue.

Now you will remove (erase) the file from the screen and retrieve the worksheet from the disk.

**Press:** [/]

**Select:** **Worksheet, Erase, Yes**

The screen should be blank. Now retrieve the disk file.

**Press:**     $\boxed{/}$

**Select:**     **File, Retrieve**

The Lotus 1-2-3 program can display five file names, in alphabetical order, on the third row of the control panel. If you have more than five worksheets saved on disk, pressing $\boxed{\downarrow}$ will display five more names. Press $\boxed{\uparrow}$ or $\boxed{\downarrow}$ until the desired file name is in the display in the control panel. Move the highlight to TRAVEL.

**Press:**     $\boxed{\text{Enter}}$

The file called TRAVEL should be back in internal memory, ready for use.

# Printing the Worksheet

Prior to printing the file, you should make certain your printer is turned on and ready. If you have a dot-matrix printer, make sure the paper is positioned so that printing will begin at the top of a sheet.

You are going to use the Print menu. It will ask what range of cells you want to print.

**Press:**     $\boxed{/}$

**Select:**     **Print, Printer, Range**

**Type:**     **A1.G17 (the range to be printed)**

**Press:**     $\boxed{\text{Enter}}$

**Select:**     **Align, Go**

When the mode indicator changes from WAIT to MENU, continue.

**Select:**     **Page, Quit**

In regard to printing a worksheet:

| The Menu Selection(s) | Tells Lotus 1-2-3 |
| --- | --- |
| Print, Printer | To send the worksheet to the printer |
| Range | To set the specified range |
| Align | Where the top of the page is |
| Go | To begin printing |
| Page | To advance the paper |
| Quit | To erase the Print menu |

# Quitting Lotus 1-2-3

Prior to exiting the program, always make sure you have saved the worksheet. Then

**Press:**     / 

**Select:**     **Quit, Yes**

# 3

- Understand the importance of budgeting
- Understand the purpose of a cash flow statement
- Indent subheadings
- Insert a blank row
- Use pointing to copy data
- Add and copy underscores
- Distinguish absolute and relative addresses
- Enter and format a date
- Sort, replace, and print a worksheet

# Preparing a Budget

Those who own and work in small businesses can't afford to make mistakes with their company's money. Since small businesses can't usually afford to hire experts to manage the financial aspects, a spreadsheet program can be a valuable tool for keeping financial data in an easy-to-use form. Spreadsheets make it easier to work and rework numbers than do paper financial statements. Built-in formulas automatically recalculate totals, averages, and the like.

This lesson introduces the basics of using Lotus 1-2-3 to prepare a budget. Your budget is your business game plan. It provides guidelines for revenue and expenses. It can be used to point out periods with cash flow problems. It provides you with a document by which you can make decisions and compare desired data to actual results. By comparing beginning-of-the-month projections with end-of-the-month results, the business person can adjust the business plan in a rational way.

A formal **cash flow statement** is a document that provides a summary of cash receipts and cash payments for a period of time, such as a month or year. It provides useful information about a company's ability to generate cash from operations, maintain and expand operating capacity, and meet financial obligations. A cash flow statement is useful to investors, creditors, and others in assessing the firm's profit potential. In addition, it provides a basis for assessing the ability of the firm to pay maturing debt. This lesson won't guide you in developing a cash flow statement, per se, but the budget this lesson will help you create can be used to evaluate a company's cash flow problems. Appendix C includes a sample of a cash flow statement. Take a look at the cash flow statement in Appendix C so you'll be familiar with the general look of a finished document.

If you haven't already loaded Lotus 1-2-3 into the internal memory of your computer, do so now.

# Indenting Subheads

When you looked at the cash flow statement in Appendix C, did you notice that subheadings were indented? A convenient way to provide indentation for subheadings is to make column A three characters wide. Major headings will start in column A and subheadings will start in column B; the result will be subheadings that look indented. To change the width of column A to 3:

| | |
|---|---|
| **Move to:** | **A1** |
| **Press:** | / |
| **Select:** | **Worksheet, Column, Set-Width** |
| **Type:** | **3** |
| **Press:** | Enter |

To change the width of column B to 19:

| | |
|---|---|
| **Move to:** | **B1** |
| **Press:** | / |

| Select: | **W**orksheet, **C**olumn, **S**et-Width |
|---------|------------------------------------------|
| **Type:** | 19 |
| **Press:** | Enter |

# Entering Budget Data

Type the following data in the cells indicated, including label prefixes as shown:

| A1 | **BUDGET FOR FIRST QUARTER 1994** |
|----|-----------------------------------|
| A3 | **EXPENSES** |
| B4 | **RENT** |
| B5 | **OFFICE SUPPLIES** |
| B6 | **RECEPTIONIST SALARY** |
| B7 | **PAYROLL TAX** |
| B8 | **PHONE** |
| B9 | **BANK SERVICE CHARGE** |
| B10 | **UTILITIES** |
| B11 | **ADVERTISING** |
| B12 | **LICENSES/PERMITS** |
| B13 | **PROFESSIONAL DUES** |
| B14 | **MISCELLANEOUS EXP** |
| B16 | **"TOTAL EXPENSES** |
| A18 | **REVENUE** |
| A20 | **SURPLUS (DEFICIT)** |
| C2 | **"JAN.** |
| D2 | **"FEB.** |

| | |
|---|---|
| E2 | "MAR. |
| F2 | "TOTAL |
| G2 | "PERCENT |

# Inserting a Blank Row

You forgot an expense item! The expense LIABILITY INSURANCE belongs between UTILITIES and ADVERTISING. To make the correction, you will begin by moving to the cell you want to move down.

| | |
|---|---|
| **Move to:** | **cell B11** |
| **Press:** | /  |
| **Select:** | **Worksheet, Insert, Row** |
| **Press:** | Enter |

This moves everything down and inserts a blank row at row 11.

| | |
|---|---|
| **Type:** | LIABILITY INSURANCE |

If necessary, you can also delete rows and columns. The menu sequence for doing so is Worksheet, Delete.

When deleting rows or columns, do not delete a row or column that contains data that a formula somewhere in the worksheet requires. If you do, the cell that contains the formula will display the message ERR.

Save your worksheet to disk before deleting columns or rows. Saving will protect you from inadvertent data loss. If you do delete data by mistake, retrieve it by using the UNDO feature ( Alt - F4 ), if the feature is available on your system.

It is a good idea to save your worksheet to disk prior to deleting columns or rows. Then, if the deletion causes problems with formulas, you have the original copy on disk. Another way to retrieve the prior version of a worksheet is to use the UNDO feature. If your system has the UNDO feature available, you can return to the previous copy of the worksheet by pressing Alt - F4 .

Your worksheet should look like *Figure 3.1.*

Figure 3.1

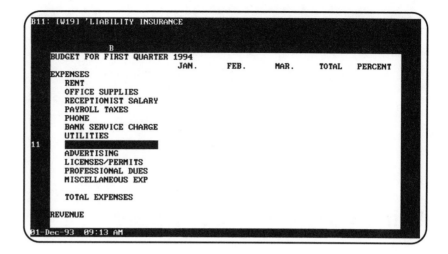

# Entering Numbers and Formulas

Enter the following numbers in the Jan. column:

| | |
|---|---|
| C4 | **800** |
| C5 | **75** |
| C6 | **450** |
| C7 | **85** |
| C8 | **120** |
| C9 | **25** |
| C10 | **285** |
| C12 | **200** |
| C13 | **500** |
| C15 | **50** |

To calculate a total at the bottom of column C:

**Move to:**     **cell C17**

**Type:**        **@SUM(C4.C16)**

The total revenue in cell C19 should be 2800.

| | |
|---|---|
| **Move to:** | **cell C19** |
| **Type:** | **2800** |

The formula in cell C21 should subtract the total expenses from the total revenue.

| | |
|---|---|
| **Move to:** | **cell C21** |
| **Type:** | **+C19−C17** |

# Using Pointing to Copy Data

Some of the data in the JAN. column is constant and will remain the same for all three months. You are going to copy the data in cells C4 through C9 to cells D4 through E9.

| | |
|---|---|
| **Move to:** | **cell C4** |
| **Press:** | ⑂ |
| **Select:** | **Copy** |

You are going to indicate the range by using a technique called pointing. **Pointing** involves using the cell pointer to highlight the range instead of typing the range. If you look at the control panel, it is asking for the range of cells to be copied.

| | |
|---|---|
| **Move to:** | **cell C9 (to highlight the range C4 through C9)** |
| **Press:** | Enter |

The question now in the control panel asks where to copy the data to.

| | |
|---|---|
| **Move to:** | **cell D4** |
| **Type:** | **. (a period)** |

This anchors the range starting at cell D4. **Anchoring** lets Lotus 1-2-3 know that you are finished typing the beginning address of the cells that define the target range. Now you will highlight the range D4 through E9.

**Move to:**     **cell E9**

**Press:**     Enter

Pointing provides a fast way to duplicate data. Now type the following data in the cells indicated:

|       |       |
|-------|-------|
| D10   | **250** |
| E10   | **200** |
| D11   | **700** |
| D12   | **300** |
| E12   | **500** |
| D14   | **200** |
| D15   | **50**  |
| E15   | **50**  |

Your spreadsheet should now look like *Figure 3.2*.

*Figure 3.2*

```
E15: 50
                                            E
                        JAN.    FEB.    MAR.    TOTAL   PERCENT
        EXPENSES
          RENT              800     800     800
          OFFICE SUPPLIES    75      75      75
          RECEPTIONIST SALARY 450    450     450
          PAYROLL TAXES       85      85      85
          PHONE              120     120     120
          BANK SERVICE CHARGE 25      25      25
          UTILITIES          205     250     200
          LIABILITY INSURANCE         700
          ADVERTISING        200     300     500
          LICENSES/PERMITS   500
          PROFESSIONAL DUES           200
    15    MISCELLANEOUS EXP   50       50  ▮▮▮▮▮▮▮▮▮

          TOTAL EXPENSES     2590

        REVENUE              2800

        SURPLUS (DEFICIT)     210
    01-Dec-93  09:15 AM
```

# Adding and Copying Underscores and Formulas

The budget would look nicer if you added some underscores, or lines that appear under data elements. This can be done by using the backslash key, ⟨\⟩, to enter the **repeat code**. The repeat code is a message to Lotus 1-2-3. It tells the program to repeat, in the cell, any character typed after ⟨\⟩. You will use the underscore character (the "Shift" of the hyphen key) to form a solid line.

| | |
|---|---|
| **Move to:** | **cell C16** |
| **Press:** | ⟨\⟩ |
| **Press:** | ⟨Shift⟩-⟨–⟩ |
| **Press:** | ⟨Enter⟩ |

Now you will create a double "underscore" by using the equals sign.

| | |
|---|---|
| **Move to:** | **cell C18** |
| **Press:** | ⟨\⟩ |
| **Press:** | ⟨=⟩ |
| **Press:** | ⟨Enter⟩ |

Now, applying what you have learned in this section, use ⟨Shift⟩-⟨–⟩ to create an underscore in cell C20 and ⟨=⟩ to create a double underscore in cell C22.

The formulas and lines in cells C16 through C22 can be copied to cells D16 through F22.

| | |
|---|---|
| **Press:** | ⟨\⟩ |
| **Select:** | **Copy** |
| **Type:** | C16.C22 |
| **Press:** | ⟨Enter⟩ |
| **Type:** | D16.F22 |
| **Press:** | ⟨Enter⟩ |

You need a formula in cell F19 to total the revenue.

| | |
|---|---|
| **Move to:** | **cell F19** |
| **Type:** | @SUM(C19.E19) |

In addition, you need a formula in cell F4 to total the three months of rent.

| | |
|---|---|
| **Move to:** | **cell F4** |
| **Type:** | @SUM(C4.E4) |
| **Press:** | Enter |

With the highlight on cell F4, copy the formula by completing these steps:

| | |
|---|---|
| **Press:** | / |
| **Select:** | **C**opy |
| **Press:** | Enter |
| **Type:** | F5.F15 |
| **Press:** | Enter |

Look at the @SUM function in the control panel.

| | |
|---|---|
| **Move to:** | **cell F5** |

Look at the control panel, noting that the cell cited is F5. Lotus 1-2-3 automatically modified the @SUM addresses to add up the data in row 5. This handy feature allows you to type the formula once and copy it to cells that use a similar formula.

# Learning About Absolute and Relative Addresses

The worksheet is now complete except for the PERCENT column. The percentage of the total expenses that each item represents can be calculated by dividing the total expense of an item by the total expense for all items.

| | |
|---|---|
| **Move to:** | **cell G4** |

| Type: | +F4/$F$17 |
|---|---|
| Press: | Enter |

Why include the dollar signs? They make the second part of the formula an absolute address. An **absolute address** cannot be changed if the formula is copied. You can copy the formula +F4/$F$17 down column G and each formula will divide the cell to its left by F17. When you type formula addresses without dollar signs, they are referred to as relative addresses. When a formula is copied, a **relative address** in the formula is modified according to the location of the formula. For further information on absolute and relative addressing, see Appendix A.

Now you will copy the formula from cell G4 to cells G5 through G15. Make sure the highlight is in cell G4.

| Press: | / |
|---|---|
| Select: | **Copy** |
| Press: | Enter |
| Type: | G5.G15 |
| Press: | Enter |

# Formatting the Worksheet

Formatting will improve the appearance of the worksheet. You will add dollar signs and percent signs to appropriate numbers.

| Move to: | cell C4 |
|---|---|
| Press: | / |
| Select: | **Range, Format, Currency** |
| Type: | 0  (to indicate your desire to have 0 decimal places) |
| Press: | Enter |
| Move to: | cell F21 (to highlight the range to be formatted) |

Press:       [Enter] (to confirm that you want a dollar sign to appear in front of each number in the defined range)

Move to:    cell G4

Press:       [/]

Select:      **R**ange, **F**ormat, **P**ercent

Type:       1 (to indicate your desire to have 1 decimal place display)

Press:       [Enter]

Move to:    cell G15 (to highlight the range to be formatted)

Press:       [Enter] (to confirm that you want a percent sign to appear after each number in the defined range)

Your screen should now look like *Figure 3.3*.

*Figure 3.3*

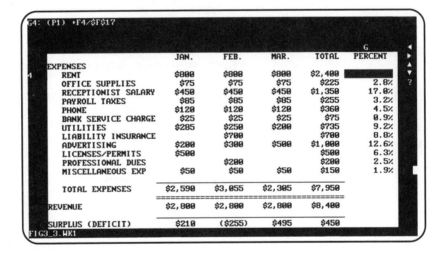

# Entering and Formatting a Date

You can put a function in a cell to tell Lotus 1-2-3 to enter the current date any time the worksheet is retrieved from disk. This function is the **@NOW function.**

| | |
|---|---|
| **Move to:** | cell E1 |
| **Type:** | @NOW |
| **Press:** | Enter |

This function displays what is called the Lotus serial date, the number of days since January 1, 1900. The reason Lotus 1-2-3 uses serial dates is so you can do math with dates. However, at the moment, you simply want to display a date in MM/DD/YY format. With the highlight still in cell E1:

| | |
|---|---|
| **Press:** | / |
| **Select:** | **Range, Format, Date** |
| **Type:** | 4 |
| **Press:** | Enter |

You have selected date format 4, which is the MM/DD/YY format.

Each time you retrieve this file from disk to make changes in it, it will display the current date.

# Sorting Data

Normally, budget items are displayed in order of size, with miscellaneous expense last regardless of size. By using Lotus 1-2-3 to sort data, you can put your worksheet in this order. To sort the data you will:

1. Highlight all columns and rows in the data range. The **data range** is all the cells to be moved around when sorting. In this case, the data range consists of cells B4 through G14. This includes all expense items except those in the category MISCELLANEOUS EXPENSE.

2. Indicate which column is the **sort key**, the field by which you are sorting.

Sorting data can mess up your worksheet if you don't do it right. So, save the file to disk just before sorting. Then, if you mess up the worksheet, you can erase the sorted worksheet, retrieve the unsorted one from disk, and try again.

3. Indicate if the sort is to arrange items in ascending or descending order. In **ascending order** items are arranged from lowest to highest. In **descending order** they are arranged from highest to lowest.

To save the file to disk, name the file BUDGET:

| | |
|---|---|
| **Press:** | ⁄ |
| **Select:** | **File, Save** |
| **Type:** | **BUDGET** |
| **Press:** | Enter |

Now you are going to sort the file:

| | |
|---|---|
| **Press:** | ⁄ |
| **Select:** | **Data, Sort** |

Mark the data range:

| | |
|---|---|
| **Select:** | **Data-Range (to mark the data range)** |

Notice that you did not include the row containing MISCELLANEOUS EXP in the data range. You did not include it because you do not want to move it.

| | |
|---|---|
| **Type:** | B4.G14 |

Next indicate the key field.

If your system has the UNDO feature available, you can return to the previous copy of the worksheet by pressing Alt - F4 . This is handy if you did not implement the sort you really wanted.

| | |
|---|---|
| **Select:** | **Primary-Key (to indicate the key field)** |
| **Move to:** | **cell F4** |
| **Press:** | Enter |
| **Type:** | D (to indicate that you want descending order) |
| **Press:** | Enter |
| **Select:** | **Go (to tell the system to start sorting)** |

Your worksheet should look like *Figure 3.4.*

*Figure 3.4*

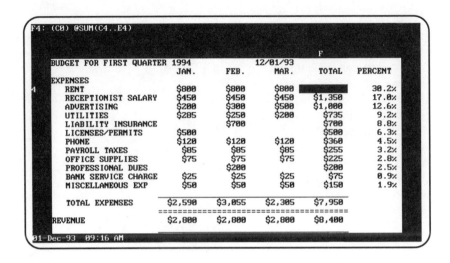

# Printing the Worksheet

Now you will save the sorted version of the worksheet.

| Press: | / |
|---|---|
| Select: | **File, Save** |
| Press: | Enter |
| Select: | **Replace** |

The reason you had to select Replace was that Lotus 1-2-3 was warning you that a file by that name already existed on the disk. When you selected Replace, you told Lotus 1-2-3 to overwrite the existing disk file, saving the current version of the file.

To print the worksheet:

| Press: | / |
|---|---|
| Select: | **Print, Printer, Range** |
| Type: | **A1.G22** |
| Press: | Enter |
| Select: | **Align, Go, Quit** |

# Quitting Lotus 1-2-3

To quit Lotus 1-2-3,

**Press:**      ⌐/⌐

**Select:**     **Quit, Yes**

With the Lotus 1-2-3 skills you have learned in this lesson, you should be able to complete a budget for yourself. Enjoy the convenience of working with an electronic spreadsheet program!

# Notes

## 4
**LESSON**

# Determining Loan Payments

Suppose you have a temporary cash flow problem and must seek loans to get you through a tough time. Or, suppose you are buying a new car and want to compare the effects of different loan periods and interest rates. A spreadsheet program can help you compare different payment variables to determine the type of loan that is most acceptable to you. This illustrates the "What if" aspect of a spreadsheet program. It lets you ask "What if I do this?" "What if I do that?"

Or, you could use the "What if" capability to evaluate the cost of giving employees a raise. To do so, you could set up a spreadsheet with weekly and annual salary and tax data. Then you could try different percentages of increases to compare the costs. Yet another use of the "What if" capability would be in determining, based on different markup percentages, the potential profit on an item. This is a very important feature that can help you make informed decisions. In this lesson, you will use "What if" capabilities to assess a car loan.

# Creating a Worksheet to Assess a Loan

Type the following data in the cells indicated:

| | |
|---|---|
| A2 | **NEW CAR COST** |
| A3 | **TRADE IN** |
| A4 | **LOAN AMOUNT** |
| A5 | **MONTHS** |
| A6 | **INTEREST RATE** |
| A7 | **MONTHLY PAYMENT** |

Your next task is to change the width of column A to 20 characters wide.

| | |
|---|---|
| **Move to:** | **cell A1** |
| **Press:** | ⌿ |
| **Select:** | **Worksheet, Column, Set-Width** |
| **Type:** | **20** |
| **Press:** | Enter |

Now change the width of columns B through E to 11.

| | |
|---|---|
| **Move to:** | **cell B1** |
| **Press:** | ⌿ |
| **Select:** | **Worksheet, Column, Column-Range, Set-Width** |
| **Move to:** | **cell E1 (to highlight B1 through E1)** |
| **Press:** | Enter |
| **Type:** | **11 (to define the desired column width)** |
| **Press:** | Enter |

Your spreadsheet should look like *Figure 4.1.*

*Figure 4.1*

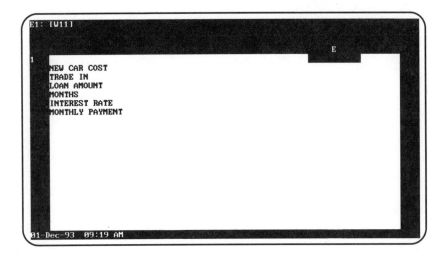

## Learning About @PMT

The **@PMT function** calculates monthly payment on a loan. You must add data to the function before it can do its work. What you must add is shown in italics:

### @PMT*(LOAN AMOUNT,INTEREST RATE,NUMBER OF PAYMENTS)*

Notice the items in the parentheses are separated by commas.

If you were trying to determine the payment on a $5,000 loan at 9.5% for 24 months, the function would read:

### @PMT(5000,.095/12,24)

Notice that there is no comma in the 5000. In @PMT, the comma is used to separate data items only. Percentages must be expressed in decimal form; therefore, 9.5% becomes .095. The second data item is divided by 12 because the 9.5% is an annual (12-month) rate. You would be making monthly payments, so the interest rate must be converted to a monthly interest rate.

If the term of the loan were being stated in years, the last data item, the monthly payment, would have to be *multiplied* by 12 to calculate the total number of payments. To determine the monthly mortgage payment on a mortgage of $55,000 at 9.5% for 30 years, you would use:

@PMT(55000,.095/12,30*12)

Type the following loan data into the worksheet:

| | |
|---|---|
| B2 | **12000** |
| B3 | **4000** |
| B4 | **+B2−B3** |
| B5 | **36** |
| B6 | **.095** |

Your next step is to enter the @PMT function in cell B7. Remember, the format is @PMT(*LOAN AMOUNT,INTEREST RATE,NUMBER OF PAYMENTS*). You can find the loan amount in cell B4; the interest rate, in cell B6; and the term of the loan, in cell B5.

| | |
|---|---|
| **Move to:** | **cell B7** |
| **Type:** | **@PMT(B4,B6/12,B5)** |

# Formatting and Using the Worksheet

Now you need to format the cells to make the worksheet more readable. First, you are going to format cells B2 through E4 for currency, with no decimal places. The reason you are going to format the cells over to column E is so you can try different alternatives.

| | |
|---|---|
| **Move to:** | **cell B2** |
| **Press:** | ⌿ |
| **Select:** | **Range, Format, Currency** |
| **Type:** | **0 (to indicate you do not want decimal places)** |
| **Press:** | Enter |
| **Move to:** | **cell E4 (to highlight the range B2 through E4)** |
| **Press:** | Enter |

Now you are going to format the interest rate as a percentage with one decimal place.

| Move to: | **cell B6** |
|---|---|
| Press: |  |
| Select: | **Range, Format, Percent** |
| Type: | **1** |
| Press: | Enter |
| Move to: | **cell E6** |
| Press: | Enter |
| Move to: | **cell B7** |
| Press: | ⁄ |
| Select: | **Range, Format, Currency** |
| Press: | Enter |
| Move to: | **cell E8** |
| Press: | Enter |

Your worksheet should look like *Figure 4.2*.

*Figure 4.2*

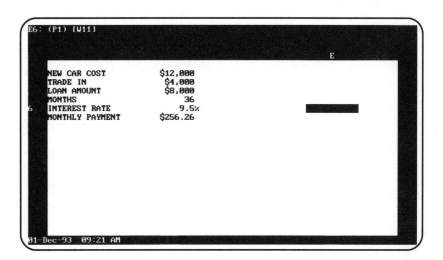

You will use pointing to copy the data and formulas in column B to columns C through E. Remember that pointing involves typing a period to anchor the cell at the beginning of the desired range. Then you simply move the cursor to highlight the range.

| | |
|---|---|
| Move to: | cell B2 |
| Press: | ⌨ / |
| Select: | **Copy** |
| Move to: | cell B7 (to highlight cells B2 through B7) |
| Press: | ⌨ Enter |
| Move to: | cell C2 |
| Type: | . (a period, to anchor the cell) |
| Move to: | cell E7 (to highlight cells C2 through E7) |
| Press: | ⌨ Enter |

Now try different interest rates and loan periods. Type the following data in the cells indicated, overwriting the current data:

C5   48

D5   60

E6   .09

Your worksheet should look like *Figure 4.3*.

Now you can compare different options. You will begin by comparing the amount of interest you would pay.

| | |
|---|---|
| Move to: | cell A8 |
| Type: | TOTAL INTEREST PAID |

The formula to calculate the total interest must multiply the monthly payment by the number of payments and, from that product, subtract the amount borrowed. (+ monthly payment * total number of payments – loan amount)

*Figure 4.3*

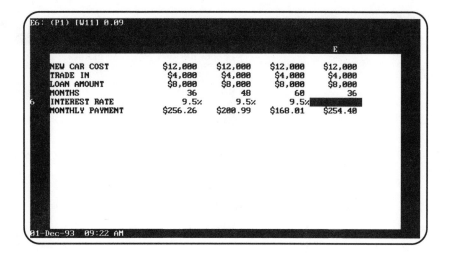

| Move to: | cell B8 |
|---|---|
| Type: | +B7*B5-B4 |

Now, to copy this formula from cell B8 to cells C8 through E8:

| Move to: | cell B8 |
|---|---|
| Press: | ⌐/⌐ |
| Select: | **C**opy |
| Press: | Enter (to indicate that the formula is to be copied from the current cell, B8) |
| Move to: | cell C8 (to indicate the destination of the formula) |
| Type: | . (a period, to anchor the range) |
| Move to: | cell E8 (to highlight the range C8 through E8) |
| Press: | Enter |

Now try some "What if" questions with mortgage figures. Type the following data in columns A and B, starting at cell A13 (A13 through B17):

| MORTGAGE | 45000 |
|---|---|
| NO. OF YEARS | 30 |

**51**

*Figure 4.4*

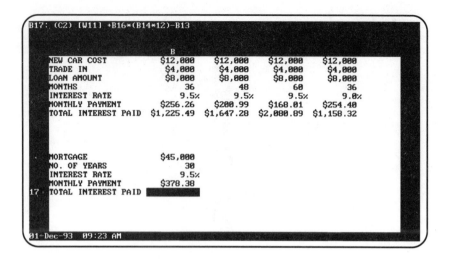

```
B17: (C2) [W11] +B16*(B14*12)-B13



              B
NEW CAR COST           $12,000    $12,000    $12,000    $12,000
TRADE IN                $4,000     $4,000     $4,000     $4,000
LOAN AMOUNT             $8,000     $8,000     $8,000     $8,000
MONTHS                      36         48         60         36
INTEREST RATE             9.5%       9.5%       9.5%       9.0%
MONTHLY PAYMENT        $256.26    $200.99    $168.01    $254.40
TOTAL INTEREST PAID  $1,225.49  $1,647.28  $2,000.89  $1,158.32




MORTGAGE              $45,000
NO. OF YEARS               30
INTEREST RATE            9.5%
MONTHLY PAYMENT       $378.38
17  TOTAL INTEREST PAID  ███████████

01-Dec-93   09:23 AM
```

INTEREST RATE                .095

MONTHLY PAYMENT

TOTAL INTEREST PAID      +B16*(B14*12)-B13

In cell B16, enter the @PMT function. The format is:

**@PMT***(LOAN AMOUNT, INTEREST RATE, NUMBER OF PAYMENTS)*

Remember, the number of payments in the @PMT is B14*12.

Format the data with the appropriate format codes. When you are done, your worksheet should look like *Figure 4.4.*

You would pay back over $135,000, with over $90,000 in interest.

Try other mortgage amounts, years, and interest rates.

# Quitting Lotus 1-2-3

To quit Lotus 1-2-3,

Press:        **/Quit, Yes**

# 5
**LESSON**

## OBJECTIVES

- Understand the importance of a balance sheet
- Understand what an asset is and the difference between current assets and fixed assets
- Understand what a liability is and the difference between current liabilities and long-term liabilities
- Explain common Lotus 1-2-3 formats: Date, Comma, Currency, General, Fixed, Percent
- Use headers and footers for page numbering

# Preparing a Balance Sheet

Eventually, even the smallest business needs a **balance sheet**. It lists the value of the **assets** (items of value the business owns), the total **liabilities** (money owed) and the **owner's equity** (assets minus liabilities) as of a specific date. It is used by lenders to determine the worth of the business. You will need a balance sheet if you want to sell a business. With a balance sheet, you can analyze assets, determine **current assets** (cash and those things that will convert into cash during one year), and **fixed assets** (those things of a "permanent" nature, usually with a life of over one year). Excluding land, fixed assets usually decline in value over time. This decline is called **depreciation**.

Additionally, a balance sheet lets you analyze debts and shows the **working capital**, the assets that can be applied to the operation of the business.

Bankers look at a balance sheet to determine the current ratio. This ratio is determined by dividing the total current assets by the total current liabilities. Another ratio commonly used is the acid-test ratio or quick ratio. This is the balance sheet ratio of total quick assets (cash and marketable securities) to total current liabilities.

A spreadsheet program can help measurably in preparation of a balance sheet.

# Setting Up a Balance Sheet

A balance sheet begins with a heading.

In cell D1:

**Type:**        JOHN DOE REAL ESTATE

In cell D2:

**Type:**        BALANCE SHEET

In cell D3:

**Type:**        DECEMBER 31, 1994

You are going to put the dollar values of the accounts in columns E, F and G, so you may as well format these columns before you enter data. (Formatting can be done either before entering data or after data is placed in a worksheet.)

**Press:**        ⌶/

**Select:**      **Range, Format, Currency**

**Press:**        ⌴Enter

**Type:**         E4.G99

**Press:**        ⌴Enter

You have now formatted more than enough rows for the numeric data.

Columns E, F, and G need to be widened to 11 characters.

**Press:**        ⌶/

**Select:**  **W**orksheet, **C**olumn, **C**olumn-Range, **S**et-Width

**Type:**  11

**Press:**  [Enter]

A balance sheet starts with a listing of the items the business owns, the current assets and fixed assets.

In cell C6:

**Type:**  ASSETS

Change the width of column A to 3 so you can use it to indent subheadings. You will list the actual items in column B.

In cell A8:

**Type:**  CURRENT ASSETS

In the rows indicated, type the following account titles in column B and the amounts in column E:

| | | |
|---|---|---|
| row 9 | CASH IN BANK | 1235.86 |
| row 10 | PETTY CASH | 50.00 |
| row 11 | SUPPLIES | 130.00 |
| row 12 | PREPAID RENT | 500.00 |

In cell C13:

**Type:**  TOTAL CURRENT ASSETS

You will put the @SUM function in cell F13 to add up the values in cells E9 through E12.

In cell F13:

**Type:**  @SUM(E9.E12)

Cell F13 should now display $1,915.86.

Now enter the heading FIXED ASSETS in cell A14. Fixed assets usually are items that depreciate over the life of the asset. You are going to type the original purchase price of each fixed asset and then subtract the depreciation accumulated to date to determine the book value of the asset.

Type the following account titles in columns B and C, and the amounts in column E:

| | | | |
|---|---|---|---|
| row 15, column B | **AUTOMOBILE** | | **14500.00** |
| row 16, column C | **LESS ACCUM. DEPR.** | | **3000.00** |
| row 18, column B | **OFFICE EQUIP** | | **3500.00** |
| row 19, column C | **LESS ACCUM. DEPR** | | **800.00** |

Now you need to total the fixed assets:

In cell C20:

> **Type:**     **TOTAL FIXED ASSETS**

In cell F20:

> **Type:**     **+E15−E16+E18−E19**

Cell F20 should display $14,200.00.

In cell A22:

> **Type:**     **TOTAL ASSETS**

In cell G22:

> **Type:**     **+F13+F20**

The total assets are $16,115.86.

To add lines above and below the total assets:

> **Move to:**   **cell G21**
>
> **Press:**    ⧵ , Shift − −
>
> **Move to:**   **cell G23**
>
> **Press:**    ⧵ , =

Your worksheet should look like *Figure 5.1.*

*Figure 5.1*

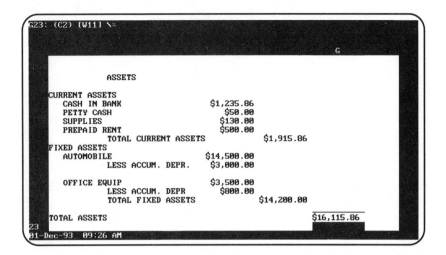

```
G23: (C2) [W11] \=
                                                                    G

              ASSETS

CURRENT ASSETS
   CASH IN BANK              $1,235.86
   PETTY CASH                   $50.00
   SUPPLIES                    $130.00
   PREPAID RENT                $500.00
            TOTAL CURRENT ASSETS          $1,915.86
FIXED ASSETS
   AUTOMOBILE                $14,500.00
         LESS ACCUM. DEPR.   $3,000.00

   OFFICE EQUIP               $3,500.00
         LESS ACCUM. DEPR      $800.00
         TOTAL FIXED ASSETS             $14,200.00

TOTAL ASSETS                              $16,115.86
23
01-Dec-93  09:26 AM
```

The next category on a balance sheet is the equity section. **Equity** is the ownership rights to the assets. Equity is split between the creditors and the owner. To add a title to this section:

**Move to:**    **cell C26**

**Type:**    **LIABILITIES AND OWNER'S EQUITY**

Just as assets were broken into current and noncurrent, so are liabilities. **Current liabilities** are considered those items that must be paid within the next year. **Long-term liabilities** are those items that won't be paid within the next year. An example would be a mortgage. A mortgage consists of the payments that you will make in the next 12 months (current liabilities) and the remainder of the mortgage (long-term liabilities).

In cell A27:

**Type:**    **CURRENT LIABILITIES**

Type the following data, entering the text in column B and the amounts in E:

| | | |
|---|---|---|
| row 28 | **PAYROLL TAXES PAYABLE** | 126.39 |
| row 29 | **CURRENTLY DUE ON LOAN** | 350.00 |
| row 30 | **ACCOUNTS PAYABLE** | 425.00 |

**57**

In cell C31:

    **Type:**        `TOTAL CURRENT LIABILITIES`

In cell F31:

    **Type:**        `@SUM(E28.E30)`

Now you need to enter the long-term liabilities.

    **Move to:**    **cell A33**

    **Type:**        `LONG TERM LIABILITIES`

    **Move to:**    **cell B34**

    **Type:**        `LOAN AT XYZ BANK`

    **Move to:**    **cell F34**

    **Type:**        `9650`

Note that you entered the value 9650 without decimal places. Recall that you have added other dollar amounts with decimal places (1235.86). Because you told Lotus 1-2-3 to use the Currency format, the program adds the zeros to 9650 automatically.

In cell C36:

    **Type:**        `TOTAL LIABILITIES`

    **Move to:**    **cell F36**

    **Type:**        `+F31+F34`

    **Move to:**    **cell A38**

    **Type:**        `OWNER'S EQUITY`

    **Move to:**    **cell B39**

    **Type:**        `JOHN DOE, CAPITAL`

The owner's equity is the total value of the assets minus what is owed to creditors.

    **Move to:**    **cell F39**

| | |
|---|---|
| **Type:** | +G22−F36 |
| **Move to:** | cell A41 |
| **Type:** | TOTAL LIABILITIES AND OWNER'S EQUITY |
| **Move to:** | cell G41 |
| **Type:** | +F36+F39 |

Cell G41 should display $16,115.86.

To add lines above and below the number in cell G41:

| | |
|---|---|
| **Press:** | ⟨\⟩, ⟨Shift⟩-⟨−⟩ |
| **Move to:** | cell G42 |
| **Press:** | ⟨\⟩, ⟨=⟩ |
| **Press:** | ⟨Enter⟩ |

Your screen should look like *Figure 5.2*.

# Formatting Numbers

You have used several formatting styles in the lessons in this book. In this lesson, you used Currency. A Lotus 1-2-3 user should be familiar with some of the other common formats.

*Figure 5.2*

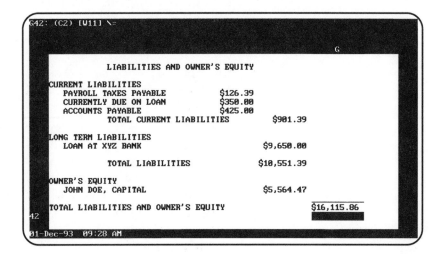

59

**Fixed.** The Fixed format controls the number of decimal places. It does *not* add a comma if the number exceeds 999. It does round to the number of decimal places you request. If you request zero decimal places and type 1.5, the number displayed is 2. The actual data in the cell is still 1.5. If you use the value in the cell in a formula, the formula uses 1.5, not 2.

**Comma.** This format does the same thing as the Fixed format, but it adds a comma when the number exceeds 999.

**Currency.** The Currency format does the same thing the Comma format does, but it adds dollar signs. It will add commas to numbers over 999. The Currency format controls the number of decimal places and rounds data if necessary. Negative numbers appear in parenthesis. For example: ($2,345.55)

**Date.** This format converts Lotus 1-2-3 serial dates to the dates we view. As you recall, January 1, 1900, is serial date 1. The Date format converts 34436 to 12-Apr-94, for example.

**Percent.** The Percent format multiplies the number in the cell by 100 to move the decimal point two places to the right, and adds a percent sign. For example, if you type .05, what appears is 5%.

The table that follows summarizes the preceding information about formats.

## FORMATTING NUMERIC DATA

| A Original Data Entered | B Fixed Format Decimal Places: 1 | C Currency Format Decimal Places: 0 | D* Date Format | E† Percent Format Decimal Places: 3 |
|---|---|---|---|---|
| 0.08 | 0.1 | $0 | *********** | 8.000% |
| 1 | 1.0 | $1 | 01-Jan-00 | 100.000% |
| 1.555 | 1.6 | $2 | 01-Jan-00 | 155.500% |
| 2.34763 | 2.3 | $2 | 02-Jan-00 | 234.763% |
| 123.321 | 123.3 | $123 | 02-May-00 | 12332.100% |
| 12483.01 | 12483.0 | $12,483 | 05-Mar-94 | *********** |

\* The date in the first row of column D is asterisks because a number less than 1 cannot be converted to a date.
† The asterisks at the bottom of column E indicate that the column is not wide enough to display the formatted data.

# Printing Headers, Footers, and Page Numbers

A **header** is a single line printed at the top of all pages. It is followed by two blank lines. A **footer** is a single line printed at the bottom of all pages, preceded by two blank lines. The data in a header or footer is not displayed in a spreadsheet cell. Lotus 1-2-3 keeps it in a separate area, not visible on the screen unless you are in the Print menu.

Headers and footers often contain the current date or the current page. Headers and footers are entered through the Print menu. You will create a footer.

**Press:**          /

**Select:**        **Print, Printer**

**Select:**        **O**ptions (to reveal the Options submenu)

**Select:**        **Footer**

At this point you can type the text of the footer that will appear on the page when the worksheet is printed.

Lotus 1-2-3 offers two codes that can be helpful in creating headers and footers. The code @ in a header or footer tells Lotus 1-2-3 to insert the current date at the spot @ appears. The code # tells Lotus 1-2-3 to enter the appropriate page numbers.

**Type:**        **PAGE #**

You have instructed Lotus 1-2-3 to print the word "PAGE" and the actual page number at the bottom of each page. The page number will be left-aligned in the footer. You could have used the vertical bar code ( ¦ , entered by pressing the "Shift" of the \ key) to tell Lotus 1-2-3 to center the text, or the double vertical bar code ( ¦ ¦ ) to tell Lotus 1-2-3 to right-align it. The list that follows presents examples that use these codes.

DATE @ ¦ XYZ COMPANY ¦ PAGE #

This left-aligns the word "DATE" and the actual date, centers COMPANY (which represents a company name in this example) and right-aligns the word "PAGE" and the actual page number.

| ¦ ¦ PAGE # | This right-aligns the word "PAGE" and the page number. |
|---|---|
| ¦ - # - | This prints a hyphen, the page number, and another hyphen in the center of the header or footer. |
| DATE @ ¦ ¦ PAGE # | This left-aligns the word "DATE" and the current date, and right-aligns the word "PAGE" and the page number. |

Now try using a few of these codes. Following PAGE #

| Type: | ¦ – # – |
|---|---|
| Press: | Enter |
| Select: | **Quit (to return to the main print menu)** |
| Select: | **Range** |
| Press: | Enter |
| Type: | **A1.G42** |
| Press: | Enter |
| Select: | **Align, Go, Page, Quit (to print the worksheet)** |

Look at the printout to see the footer.

Save your file to disk and quit Lotus 1-2-3.

# 6

## LESSON

- Understand what an income statement is and the categories that compose it

- Distinguish between the three Lotus 1-2-3 command sequences that erase data

- Distinguish between the three command sequences that save files to disk

- Know the meanings of the file extensions used by Lotus 1-2-3

# Preparing an Income Statement

An **income statement** lists revenue and expenses over a period of time, such as a month or a three-month period. Basically, it answers the question "How much money is the business making?"

An income statement starts with the **revenue**, which is the money a company earned in the process of doing business. Expenses are then listed. **Expenses** are the cost of doing business. Expenses include items such as rent, wages, telephone, insurance, depreciation, and advertising. The "bottom line" of an income statement reports the actual net income or net loss for the business during the period covered by the statement. The **net income** or net profit, is calculated by subtracting the total expenses from the total income. Income statements may be for one month, a quarter, or a year. The period covered must be indicated in the heading so the reader can interpret the data accurately.

The income statement is used by a variety of people, such as the business owner, potential creditors, and the income tax preparer. It is an essential document for the business person.

# Creating the Heading for an Income Statement

An income statement begins with a heading indicating the name of the company, the statement name, and the period of time covered by the statement. The period of time is necessary because the reader needs to know how long it took to earn the income indicated by the statement.

Type the following data in the cells indicated. (Note that cell C2 starts with two blank spaces.)

| | |
|---|---|
| C1 | **JOHN DOE REAL ESTATE** |
| C2 | **' INCOME STATEMENT** |
| B3 | **FOR MONTH ENDING APRIL 30, 1995** |

# Defining Column Width and Format

You are going to change the column width and formats to prepare for entering data. The width of column A will be 4.

| | |
|---|---|
| **Move to:** | **any cell in column A** |
| **Press:** | ⃞/ |
| **Select:** | **Worksheet, Column, Set-Width** |
| **Type:** | **4** |
| **Press:** | ⃞Enter |

Also, you need to change the width of columns E and F to 11 so they can hold large numbers. Since they are two adjacent columns, you can change both at the same time.

| | |
|---|---|
| **Move to:** | **any cell in column E** |
| **Press:** | ⃞/ |
| **Select:** | **Worksheet, Column, Column-Range, Set-Width** |

| | |
|---|---|
| **Move:** | **One cell to the right (to indicate that the width of columns E and F will be modified)** |
| **Press:** | Enter |
| **Type:** | **11** |
| **Press:** | Enter |

Now you will implement Currency format with two decimal places. The cells to be formatted are the ones in column E and F. Since you are not sure how many rows you will need, you are going to format all cells from E7 through F99.

| | |
|---|---|
| **Press:** | / |
| **Select:** | **Range, Format, Currency** |
| **Press:** | Enter |
| **Type:** | **E7.F99** |
| **Press:** | Enter |

Your screen should look like *Figure 6.1.* Note the display in the control panel, which indicates the characteristics of cell E7. C2 indicates that the format is Currency, two decimal places. W11 indicates that the column width is 11 characters.

*Figure 6.1*

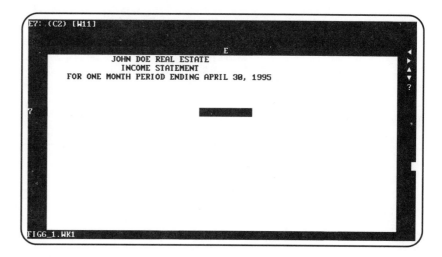

65

# Entering Income Data

A business can have several types of income. Income derived solely from the operation of a business is called **operating income**. **Nonoperating** income, or other income, is derived from sources other than normal business functions. Examples of nonoperating income are rent from an apartment on the second floor of a building owned by a barbershop, interest income earned from loans to employees, or interest on customers' charge accounts or bank deposits.

An income statement starts with income earned from the primary function of the business it describes.

    Move to:    cell A6

Type the following data in the cells indicated

| | |
|---|---|
| A6 | **REVENUE** |
| B7 | **COMMISSION INCOME** |
| E7 | **12000** |
| C8 | **TOTAL REVENUE** |
| F8 | **+E7** |

Cell F8 now displays the gross profit. **Gross profit** is the total profit before expenses, or the revenue. As you have already learned, net income (or net profit) is calculated by subtracting the total expenses from the gross profit. A business could have a gross profit of $10,000 but a net loss of $2,000 because the expenses were $12,000.

# Erasing Data

What do you do if you make a mistake and want to erase the data and start over? Lotus 1-2-3 offers three methods you should be familiar with.

### Using File, Erase

Selecting the sequence File, Erase enables you to erase a disk file from the disk. When you select this sequence, Lotus 1-2-3 displays a list of files saved on the disk. You simply move the highlight to the appropriate file name and press Enter. Lotus 1-2-3 will ask you if you want to erase the file; you must select Yes or No from the menu. If you select Yes from the menu, the file will no longer be available on the disk. The unavailability is permanent—even the UNDO command cannot reverse it—so be certain you really want to erase the disk file.

### Using Worksheet, Erase

The sequence Worksheet, Erase enables you to erase the entire worksheet displayed on the screen. The worksheet is erased from internal memory (RAM). If the worksheet is saved on disk prior to this operation, the disk file is unaffected by the Worksheet, Erase sequence. This sequence can be reversed with UNDO (Alt-F4).

### Using Range, Erase

Selecting the sequence Range, Erase enables you to erase a range of cells in the current worksheet on the screen (in RAM). This sequence clears the indicated cells. It affects internal memory (RAM) only. This command can be reversed with UNDO (Alt-F4).

# Entering Operating Expenses and Income

The next category on the income statement should list the expenses from normal business operations. Expenses incurred during the normal operation of a business are referred to as **operating expenses**. Expenses such as interest on a mortgage and fines or penalties are considered **nonoperating expenses**. They do not occur in the normal course of business. (Interest expense is a cost of financing.)

Operating expenses are listed on an income statement in order of size, from largest to smallest, except for Miscellaneous expenses. Miscellaneous expenses are lumped in a single category and listed last, regardless of size.

In cell A10:

Type:  **OPERATING EXPENSES**

Then, starting in row 11, column B, type the following expense categories and, in column E, the following amounts:

| | |
|---|---|
| RENT | 800 |
| CAR | 800 |
| LICENSES/PERMITS | 500 |
| RECEPTIONIST SALARY | 450 |
| UTILITIES | 285 |
| ADVERTISING | 200 |
| PHONE | 120 |
| PAYROLL TAXES | 85 |
| OFFICE SUPPLIES | 75 |
| BANK SERVICE CHARGES | 25 |
| MISCELLANEOUS EXPENSE | 50 |

The cells from B11 through E21 should now be filled.

In cell C23:

Type:  **TOTAL OPERATING EXPENSES**

Now you must place a formula in cell F23 to have Lotus 1-2-3 add up the total of all the expenses. You will use pointing to enter the @SUM function in cell F23.

Move to:  **cell F23**

Type:  **@SUM(**

Move to:  **cell E11**

Type:  **. (a period, to anchor the range)**

**Move to:** cell E21

**Type:** ) (a right parenthesis)

**Press:** Enter

The next step is to draw a line under the expense figure.

**Move to:** cell F24

**Press:** \, Shift-−, Enter

Your screen should look like *Figure 6.2*.

The worksheet needs a label in cell A25 to indicate that this line will contain the net income.

**Move to:** cell A25

**Type:** NET INCOME FROM OPERATIONS

You must enter a formula into cell F25 to calculate the actual income amount. You will use the pointing technique to define the cells the formula should use.

**Move to:** cell F25

**Type:** + (to indicate the start of a formula)

*Figure 6.2*

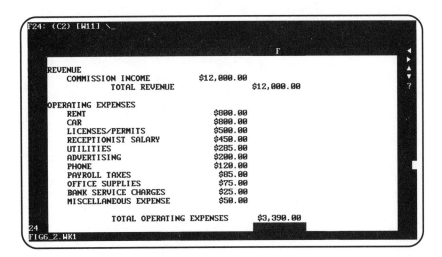

F24: (C2) [W11] \_

|                        |          F          |
|---|---|
| REVENUE |  |
| COMMISSION INCOME | $12,000.00 |
| TOTAL REVENUE | $12,000.00 |
|  |  |
| OPERATING EXPENSES |  |
| RENT | $800.00 |
| CAR | $800.00 |
| LICENSES/PERMITS | $500.00 |
| RECEPTIONIST SALARY | $450.00 |
| UTILITIES | $285.00 |
| ADVERTISING | $200.00 |
| PHONE | $120.00 |
| PAYROLL TAXES | $85.00 |
| OFFICE SUPPLIES | $75.00 |
| BANK SERVICE CHARGES | $25.00 |
| MISCELLANEOUS EXPENSE | $50.00 |
|  |  |
| TOTAL OPERATING EXPENSES | $3,390.00 |

24
FIG6_2.WK1

The net income from operations is total revenue minus total operating expenses.

**Move to:** cell F8 (note that the control panel displays +F8)

**Type:** – (to provide a minus sign)

The cell pointer jumps back to cell F25 so you can indicate the next address.

**Move to:** cell F23 (to indicate you want to subtract total operating expenses)

Look at the control panel. It contains the formula +F8–F23.

**Press:** Enter (to complete the formula)

# Saving the File to Disk

Periodically, you should save an open file to disk to provide backup in case of some problem. In the event of a power failure or hardware failure, for example, you would have a partially completed worksheet on disk for backup. Three command sequences are commonly used when dealing with disk files:

**File, Directory**

**File, Save**

**File, List**

Each sequence produces a different result. The first sequence, (File Directory) is used to check and reset the path. The path consists of directions to the appropriate spot on disk. It includes the relevant disk drive and may include a subdirectory name. Try this sequence now:

**Press:** /

**Select:** **File, Directory**

*Figure 6.3*

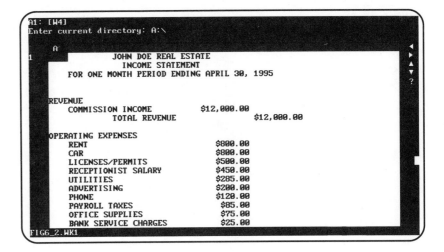

```
A1: [W4]
Enter current directory: A:\

    A
1
                    JOHN DOE REAL ESTATE
                      INCOME STATEMENT
         FOR ONE MONTH PERIOD ENDING APRIL 30, 1995


REVENUE
    COMMISSION INCOME          $12,000.00
              TOTAL REVENUE                 $12,000.00

OPERATING EXPENSES
    RENT                         $800.00
    CAR                          $800.00
    LICENSES/PERMITS             $500.00
    RECEPTIONIST SALARY          $450.00
    UTILITIES                    $285.00
    ADVERTISING                  $200.00
    PHONE                        $120.00
    PAYROLL TAXES                 $85.00
    OFFICE SUPPLIES               $75.00
    BANK SERVICE CHARGES          $25.00
FIG6_2.WK1
```

The control panel displays the path Lotus 1-2-3 will follow in executing disk commands. If C:\ appears on your screen, the path is the main (root) directory on the hard disk. If C:\123 appears, the path is to the 123 subdirectory on the hard disk, C. If A:\ appears (as in *Figure 6.3*),the path is to the root directory of the diskette in drive A. To change the path, simply type the desired path. Press Enter to complete the command.

Now consider the sequence that saves files. File, Save saves a file in the current directory or path. If the file has been previously named, Lotus 1-2-3 displays the file name. If the file to be saved is to use the same name, you would simply press Enter. Lotus 1-2-3 then asks you if you want to Replace the current file on disk by overwriting it with the updated version of the worksheet. If the name is to be changed, you would type the new name and press Enter. If the worksheet has not been saved previously, you would type a file name and press Enter. *Figure 6.4* shows how the control panel would look after a new file name were typed.

The sequence File, List looks at a list of files saved in the current directory. After the File, List sequence is selected, Lotus 1-2-3 asks what type of files you wish to list. If you select Other, all files in the path are displayed. If you select Worksheet, only files that have an extension starting with the characters .WK are displayed. The list that follows discusses these extensions.

*Figure 6.4*

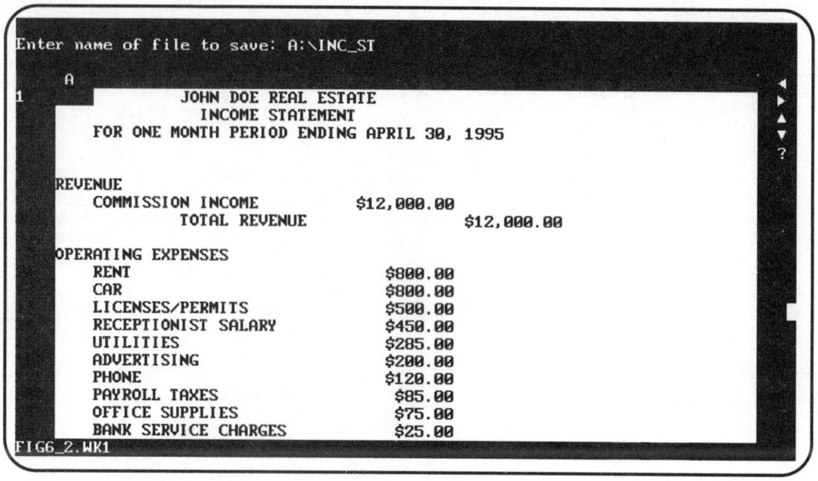

```
Enter name of file to save: A:\INC_ST

     A
1              JOHN DOE REAL ESTATE
               INCOME STATEMENT
       FOR ONE MONTH PERIOD ENDING APRIL 30, 1995


     REVENUE
       COMMISSION INCOME          $12,000.00
                TOTAL REVENUE                $12,000.00

     OPERATING EXPENSES
       RENT                        $800.00
       CAR                         $800.00
       LICENSES/PERMITS            $500.00
       RECEPTIONIST SALARY         $450.00
       UTILITIES                   $285.00
       ADVERTISING                 $200.00
       PHONE                       $120.00
       PAYROLL TAXES                $85.00
       OFFICE SUPPLIES              $75.00
       BANK SERVICE CHARGES         $25.00
FIG6_2.WK1
```

**.WKS** indicates a file saved with Lotus 1-2-3 release 1A.

**.WK1** indicates a file saved with Lotus 1-2-3 release 2.

**.WK3** indicates a file saved with Lotus 1-2-3 release 3.

**.WK4** indicates a file saved with Lotus 1-2-3 for Windows, release 4.

When you execute the sequence File, List, Other or the sequence File, List, Worksheet, a list of file names appears on the screen. Pressing [Enter] redisplays the current worksheet. Remember, this only *displays* a list of saved files. You cannot retrieve a file from this display. If you see a file you want to read into RAM, you must press [Enter] and then use the File, Retrieve sequence.

The income statement you have created should be saved to disk.

**Press:**       [/]

**Select:**     **File, Save**

**Type:**        INC_ST

**Press:**       [Enter]

# Entering Nonoperating Expenses and Income

Now you need to type data in regard to nonoperating expenses and nonoperating income. Type the following data in the cells indicated:

| | |
|-----|-----|
| A27 | **OTHER EXPENSES** |
| B28 | **INTEREST EXPENSE** |
| E28 | **94.26** |
| B29 | **FINES AND PENALTIES** |
| E29 | **200** |
| F30 | **@SUM(E28.E29)** |
| A31 | **OTHER INCOME** |
| B32 | **INTEREST ON LOAN TO EMPLOYEE** |
| F32 | **85** |
| A34 | **NET INCOME** |
| F34 | **+F25-F30+F32** |

Draw a line above and below the net income figure in F34 by taking the following steps:

| | |
|----------|----------|
| **Move to:** | **cell F33** |
| **Press:** | \boxed{\}, \boxed{Shift}-\boxed{-} **(to type an underscore)** |
| **Move to:** | **cell F35** |
| **Press:** | \boxed{\}, \boxed{Shift}-\boxed{=} **(to type a double underscore)** |

Your screen should look like *Figure 6.5*.

The income statement is now complete. Take the steps that follow to save it to disk.

*Figure 6.5*

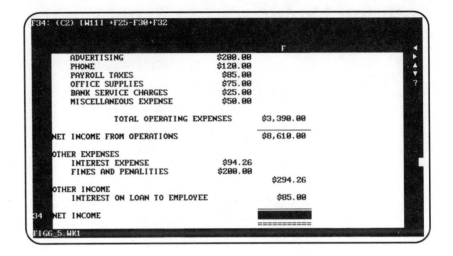

| Press: | / |
| --- | --- |
| Select: | **F**ile, **S**ave |
| Press: | Enter |
| Select: | **R**eplace |

Take the steps that follow to print the worksheet.

| Press: | / |
| --- | --- |
| Select: | **P**rint, **P**rinter, **R**ange |
| Type: | A1.F35 |
| Press: | Enter |
| Select: | **A**lign, **G**o, **P**age, **Q**uit |

# 7

## OBJECTIVES

- Set X and A data
- Use the automatic fill feature to shade "slices" of a pie chart
- Explode a piece of a pie chart
- View charts and graphs
- Add a title to a pie chart
- Save charts and graphs
- Use a release 2 or release 3 version of Lotus 1-2-3 to print a chart
- Create a bar graph
- Add legends to a graph

Users of Lotus 1-2-3 release 2: to load the program if you will be printing graphs, type LOTUS and then select 1-2-3.

# Drawing Charts and Graphs

A picture is worth a thousand words. The purpose of this lesson is to demonstrate how financial data in columns can be converted into graphic displays. Sales data for a period of time is easier to analyze in a graph than in a table.

To print graphs, release 2 users must start up the Lotus 1-2-3 program by typing LOTUS instead of 123. The next step is to select 1-2-3 from the menu, to enter the spreadsheet program.

In this lesson, you will create a pie chart and a bar graph. You will begin with the pie chart.

# Entering Data for a Pie Chart

In order to draw a chart, you first need some data in the worksheet. You are going to prepare a worksheet with monthly sales data for a grocery store. Type the following sales data, starting at cell A1. Type the text in column A and the numbers in column B.

| | |
|---|---|
| GROCERIES | 1200 |
| PRODUCE | 600 |
| DAIRY | 700 |
| MEAT | 4000 |
| FROZEN FOOD | 1800 |
| SUNDRIES | 1100 |

Each number in column B represents a weekly sales figure for the department cited in column A.

To widen column A to 12 characters:

| | |
|---|---|
| Press: | Home (to move the cursor to cell A1) |
| Press: | / |
| Select: | **Worksheet, Column, Set-Width** |
| Type: | 12 |
| Press: | Enter |

# Drawing a Pie Chart

A pie chart needs two sets of data. The first data series is referred to as the **X data**. This is the data that will be used to label each "slice" in a pie chart, or the bars in a bar graph. In the current example, the X data consists of the department names in column A. The second data series is referred to as the **A data**. The A data is used to determine the size of each slice in a pie chart or each bar in a bar graph. In the current example, the A data consists of the sales data in column B.

To draw a graph:

**Press:**

**Select:** **G**raph, **T**ype, **P**ie

**Select:** **X**

**Type:** **A1.A6**

**Press:** ⌷Enter⌷

**Select:** **A**

**Type:** **B1.B6**

**Press:** ⌷Enter⌷

Your screen should now look like *Figure 7.1.*

**Select:** **View**

When you are ready to return to the worksheet menu, press ⌷Enter⌷. To return to the READY mode:

**Select:** **Quit**

You can add shading to the pie chart by using the numbers in column C to indicate the type of shading. The codes you will use for shading are the numbers 2 through 7. Each number represents

*Figure 7.1*

![Graph Settings screen. A5: [W12] 'FROZEN FOODS. Menu: X A B C D E F Reset View Save Options Name Group Quit / Line Bar XY Stack-Bar Pie HLCO Mixed Features. Graph Settings dialog with Type (Pie selected), Ranges (X: [A1..A6], A: [B1..B6]), Orientation (Vertical selected), Zero line, Frame, Grid lines. FIG7_1.WK1]()

a different form of grid, or shading, in a piece of the pie. Instead of typing a set of sequential numbers, you are going to use the **automatic fill feature**. This is a feature that allows you to indicate a range to fill, the start value, and the increment. (The start value is the starting number in a series of numbers being entered with the Data, Fill command.) Lotus 1-2-3 will automatically enter the data for you.

| | |
|---|---|
| **Press:** | ⟨/⟩ |
| **Select:** | **Data, Fill** |
| **Type:** | C1.C6 **(to define the range to be filled)** |
| **Press:** | ⟨Enter⟩ |
| **Type:** | 2 **(to define the start value)** |
| **Press:** | ⟨Enter⟩ |
| **Press:** | ⟨Enter⟩ **(to accept the default step or increment, of 1)** |
| **Press:** | ⟨Enter⟩ **(to accept the default stop value)** |

Now you need to go back into the Graph menu.

| | |
|---|---|
| **Press:** | ⟨/⟩ |
| **Select:** | **Graph** |

You have to tell Lotus 1-2-3 to use the B data series. The B data series for a pie chart is for shading the pieces of the pie.

| | |
|---|---|
| **Select:** | **B** |
| **Type:** | C1.C6 |
| **Press:** | ⟨Enter⟩ |
| **Select:** | **View (to see what the chart looks like)** |

After checking the graph:

| | |
|---|---|
| **Press:** | ⟨Enter⟩ |
| **Select:** | **Quit (to exit the Graph menu)** |

If one of the departments is to be emphasized, you can ask Lotus 1-2-3 to **explode** a piece of pie, or position it so it sticks out from the pie.

> **Move to:** cell C3
>
> **Type:** 104

The 100 tells Lotus 1-2-3 to explode the piece, and the 4 defines the desired shading. To redraw the graph without going to the menu:

> **Press:** [F10]

Your screen should look like *Figure 7.2*.

Notice how the data pertaining to the Dairy Department is emphasized by the exploded piece of pie.

Your pie chart needs a title. Call up the menu. Then:

> **Select:** **G**raph, **O**ptions, **T**itles, **F**irst
>
> **Type:** SMITH GROCERY
>
> **Press:** [Enter]
>
> **Select:** **T**itles
>
> **Select:** **S**econd

*Figure 7.2*

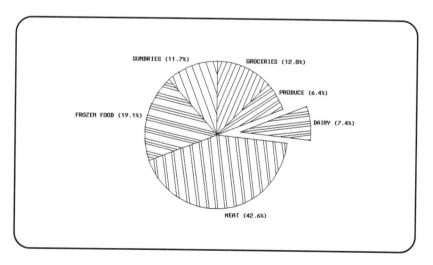

| | |
|---|---|
| Type: | SALES DATA |
| Press: | [Enter] |
| Select: | **Q**uit (to return to the main Graph menu) |
| Select: | **V**iew (to look at the revised chart) |

Remember, pressing [Enter] would return you from the view of the revised chart. Quit returns you to the Ready mode.

To save the graph to disk:

| | |
|---|---|
| Press: | [/] |
| Select: | **G**raph |
| Select: | **S**ave |
| Type: | PIE (to give the chart a file name) |
| Press: | [Enter] |

In the release 2 versions of Lotus 1-2-3, the file is saved to disk with the .PIC file name extension, instead of the normal spreadsheet extension, .WK1. In the Lotus 1-2-3 release 3 series, the graph is saved with the .CGM file name extension instead of the spreadsheet extension of .WK3.

To save the actual worksheet to disk:

| | |
|---|---|
| Press: | [/] |
| Select: | **F**ile, **S**ave |
| Type: | GRAPH (to give the worksheet a file name) |
| Press: | [Enter] |

# Printing a Pie Chart with Release 2 Versions

In order to print the chart if you use a version in the release 2 series of Lotus 1-2-3, you must enter the Lotus 1-2-3 program through the Lotus Access System menu. This allows you to access the Print Graph program. This is done by typing LOTUS at the

DOS prompt instead of 123. After you have created the chart and are ready to print it, exit the Lotus 1-2-3 program:

**Press:** ⑦

**Select:** **Quit, Yes**

Your screen should display the Lotus Access System menu. If you exited the Lotus 1-2-3 program to the DOS prompt (A:\> or C:\>), type LOTUS to restart the program.

**Move the highlight to:** **Print Graph**

Your screen should look like *Figure 7.3*.

**Press:** [Enter] **(to enter the PrintGraph program)**

Look at the settings that have appeared. Which graphs directory did you save your graph to, A or C? If the directory shown under HARDWARE SETTINGS is not the one you need:

**Select:** **Settings, Hardware, Graph-Directory**

Type the letter of the drive you want (A or C) and follow it with a colon (:).

**Press:** [Enter]

**Select:** **Quit, Quit**

*Figure 7.3*

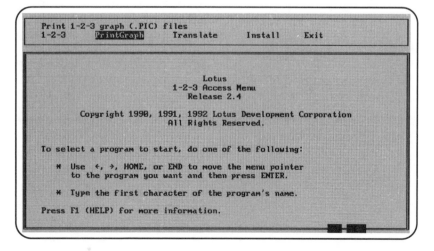

81

Figure 7.4

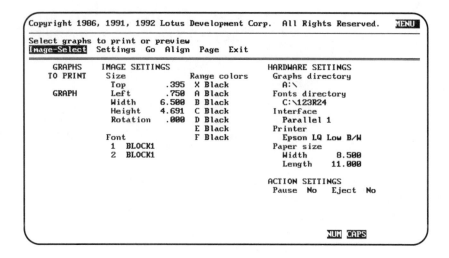

```
Copyright 1986, 1991, 1992 Lotus Development Corp.  All Rights Reserved.   MENU

Select graphs to print or preview
Image-Select  Settings  Go  Align  Page  Exit

     GRAPHS      IMAGE SETTINGS                     HARDWARE SETTINGS
    TO PRINT     Size                Range colors     Graphs directory
                 Top          .395   X Black            A:\
     GRAPH       Left         .750   A Black          Fonts directory
                 Width       6.500   B Black            C:\123R24
                 Height      4.691   C Black          Interface
                 Rotation     .000   D Black            Parallel 1
                                     E Black          Printer
                 Font                F Black            Epson LQ Low B/W
                 1  BLOCK1                            Paper size
                 2  BLOCK1                              Width      8.500
                                                        Length    11.000

                                                      ACTION SETTINGS
                                                      Pause  No   Eject  No



                                                              NUM CAPS
```

*Figure 7.4* shows the screen that results. Now you are ready to tell Lotus 1-2-3 the name of the graph you saved.

**Select:**  **Image-Select**

A list of saved graphs appear. If the only file name there is PIE, simply press [Enter]. If there are several, move the highlight down or up to the name PIE and press [Enter].

**Select:**  **Go**

The mode indicator changes to WAIT and stays that way for what seems like a long time. You cannot do anything until the mode indicator changes back to MENU. The graph should start printing. When the mode indicator displays MENU:

**Select:**  **Exit, Yes, 1-2-3 (to return to the spreadsheet program)**

# Printing a Pie Chart with Release 3 Versions

In versions of Lotus 1-2-3 series 3, you can print graphs that are part of the current spreadsheet by simply selecting the Print menu. When you get into the print menu you select Image, Current or Named, and then Align, Go, Page, Quit.

# Entering Data for a Bar and Line Graph

To try making a bar graph, you must add more data to the worksheet. In columns C and D, starting in cell C1, add the following data to the categories indicated:

| | | |
|---|---|---|
| GROCERIES | 1400 | 1300 |
| PRODUCE | 800 | 900 |
| DAIRY | 400 | 600 |
| MEAT | 3000 | 3500 |
| FROZEN FOODS | 2000 | 1700 |
| SUNDRIES | 1200 | 1000 |

Now go back into the Graph menu:

**Press:** ⌷

**Select:** **Graph**

Set up a third data:

**Select:** **C**

**Type:** D1.D6

**Press:** Enter

Look at the screen. The range for the X, A, B, and C data are set correctly, but the type of graph is still pie.

**Select:** **Type**

**Select:** **Bar (from the choices)**

View the graph now. Wouldn't it be easier to read if you added Legends? A **legend** identifies which column of data a bar represents. To add legends:

**Select:** **Options, Legend, A**

**Type:** JAN.

**Press:** Enter

83

| Select: | **Legend, B** |
|---------|---------------|
| Type: | **FEB** . |
| Press: | Enter |
| Select: | **Legend, C** |
| Type: | **MAR** . |
| Press: | Enter |

Quit this menu and View the graph. Your screen should look like *Figure 7.5.*

Try selecting the graph type Stacked-Bar, viewing the graph, and selecting the graph type Line and viewing the graph.

In order to print any graph, you would follow the steps described earlier in this lesson for printing the pie chart. Lotus 1-2-3 release 2 users must exit the 1-2-3 program and use the PrintGraph program. Lotus 1-2-3 release 3 users would print the graph using the Image submenu of the Print menu.

To exit the Lotus 1-2-3 program, make sure you have saved everything, then select Quit, Yes from the menu.

This provides an overview of the graphic capabilities of Lotus 1-2-3. There are many other features you can use in Lotus graphs. See your user's guide for details.

*Figure 7.5*

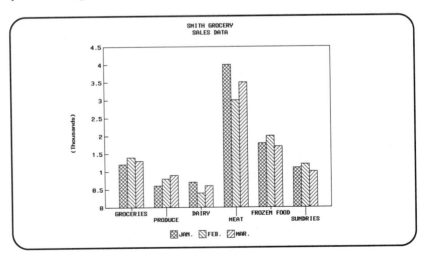

# APPENDIX A

# Understanding Different Types of Addresses

For the most part, Lotus 1-2-3 refers to cell addresses in a formula as either relative or absolute. The difference regards what happens when the formula is copied. First consider relative addresses. If the formula +B3+E9 were in cell D6, it would be interpreted relative to the cell address D6. In other words, the formula +B3+B9 would be interpreted as:

### + LEFT 2 UP 3 + RIGHT 1 DOWN 3

Why? Because B3 is two cells left and three cells up from D6, and E9 is one cell right and three cells down from D6.

This allows you to copy a formula—a formula to add the values in a column, for example. When you copy the formula to the bottom of other columns, it copies relative addresses. If B45 contains @SUM(B4.B44) it is saying:

### @SUM(UP41 cells . UP 1 cell)

Because Lotus 1-2-3 copies relative addresses, you can copy the formula to columns other than column B, without bothering to change the column indicators in the range.

Type the following in the cells indicated:

|   | A | B | C | D |
|---|------|------|-------|---------|
| 1 | JAN | FEB | TOTAL | PERCENT |
| 2 | 1000 | 2000 | | |
| 3 | 2000 | 1000 | | |
| 4 | 1000 | 3000 | | |
| 5 | 2500 | 1500 | | |
| 6 | | | | |

To total the values in column A:

| | |
|---|---|
| **Move to:** | **cell A6** |
| **Type:** | @SUM(A2.A5) |

You need a similar function in cells B6 and C6. Rather than type each @SUM, you will copy the one from A6.

| | |
|---|---|
| **Press:** | ⌿ |
| **Select:** | **Copy** |
| **Type:** | **A6** |
| **Press:** | Enter |
| **Type:** | **B6.C6** |
| **Press:** | Enter |

Watch the top left corner of the control panel.

| | |
|---|---|
| **Move to:** | **cell B6** |

See how the formula changed from @SUM(A2.A5) to @SUM(B2.B5) when you copied it? This is because Lotus 1-2-3 copied the relative addresses from the formula in cell A6. @SUM(A2.A5) was interpreted as @SUM(UP4.UP1) when it was copied. This allowed you to type the formula once and copy it to many cells, thus saving a great deal of time. Now you will work with column C.

**Move to:**     **cell C2**

**Type:**     **+A2+B2**

**Press:**     Enter

The answer appears.

You have learned three ways of thinking of the contents of cell C2:

- As the actual answer, 3000

- As the formula you typed, +A2+B2

- As Lotus 1-2-3 interprets it, or + LEFT 2 + LEFT 1

To copy the formula from cell C2 to cells C3, C4, and C5:

**Press:**     /

**Select:**     **Copy**

**Type:**     **C2**

**Press:**     Enter

**Type:**     **C3.C5**

**Press:**     Enter

Watch the control panel.

**Move to:**     **cell C3**

See how the formula has changed from +A2+B2 to +A3+B3?

To display cells D2 through D5 in Percent format, with one decimal place:

**Press:**     /

| | |
|---|---|
| Select: | **Range, Format, Percent** |
| Type: | 1 |
| Press: | Enter |
| Type: | D2.D5 |
| Press: | Enter |

Your next step is to put a formula in cell D2 so the program can calculate what percentage of the total, the value in cell C6, the value in C2 is. In other words, the formula will answer this question: "What percentage of 14,000 is 3,000?"

| | |
|---|---|
| Move to: | **cell D2** |
| Type: | **+C2/C6** |

Since you asked for Percent format, a percentage should now appear.

Now consider the need for absolute addresses. Copy the formula from cell D2 to cells D3, D4, and D5:

| | |
|---|---|
| Press: | / |
| Select: | **Copy** |
| Type: | **D2** |
| Press: | Enter |
| Type: | **D3.D5** |
| Press: | Enter |

The result is the message ERR.

Why? Move the cell pointer to cell D3 and look at the control panel. Because the formula's addresses are relative, when the formula was copied, it changed the number Lotus 1-2-3 divided by. You want to divide by the total of column C, which is the value in C6. However, the modified formula is dividing by the value in C7, and C7 is blank. You are trying to divide by zero, which can't be done.

If you make the cell address absolute in the formula, it won't be changed when it is copied. If a formula is copied, Lotus 1-2-3 won't change an absolute address in that formula. You indicate an absolute address by preceding the column and row designators with a dollar sign. The formula in cell D2 should read:

**+C2/$C$6**

Then, when you copy it to D3, D4, and D5, the only part that will change will be the designator C2. The formulas in D2, D3, D4, and D5 will divide by the value in C6.

Retype the formula in D2 so it reads:

**+C2/$C$6**

Now copy the formula:

**Press:** /

**Select:** **C**opy

**Type:** **D2**

**Press:** Enter

**Type:** **D3.D5**

**Press:** Enter

## Summarizing the Relative Address Concept

Relative addresses tells Lotus 1-2-3 to copy the relative location of a cell address, not the actual cell address as stated in the formula.

+A2+B17 tells Lotus 1-2-3 to use the relative address, not the absolute address, when copying the formula.

If C12 contains the formula +A2+B17, Lotus 1-2-3 interprets the formula as:

**+ LEFT 2 UP 10 + LEFT 1 DOWN 5**

If you copy cell C12 to R36, the new address, R36, will contain +P26+Q41, because P26 is two columns left and ten rows up from R36 and Q41 is one column left and five rows down from R36.

You copied the relative addresses, not the actual addresses, from the formula in cell C12.

## Summarizing the Absolute Address Concept

When you precede both the column and the row designator with a dollar sign, the formula address becomes absolute. If you copy the formula, Lotus 1-2-3 copies the exact address you have in the formula, the absolute address; it does not change the address according to the position of the cell pointer.

If the formula is +A10/$E$12 and you copy the formula, the first address (+A10) will be adjusted for the new location because it is relative. The second address ($E$12) will be E12 anywhere you copy the formula.

# Summarizing Common Tasks

### Inputting a Label

Position the cursor in the cell where the label is to appear.

Type the appropriate label prefix if you don't want the default.

- ' for left-alignment. This is the default.

- " right-aligns the label in the cell.

- ^ centers the label in the cell.

The mode indicator changes to LABEL.

Type the label.

Press (Enter) (or an arrow key)

## Inputting a Number

Position the cursor in the cell desired.

Type the number. A number can only contain the following characters: 0 to 9, +, –, (for minus) and a decimal point.

Numbers always right-align. You cannot center or left-align numbers in a cell. If you add a label prefix to force left alignment or centering, the data will become a label and cannot be used in math calculations, such as a calculation to total the values in a column.

## Inputting a Formula

Formulas tell Lotus 1-2-3 to calculate the contents of a cell by following the instructions in the formula. Formulas start with a plus sign or a left parenthesis. For example: +B3*.07 or (B3+B4+B5)/B7 or (B4-40)*(B6*1.5)

The arithmetic operators are:

- **+** for addition

- **–** for subtraction

- **\*** for multiplication

- **/** for division

## Editing Cell Contents

Move the cell pointer to the cell you want to modify.

**Press:**      F2

Use the left arrow, right arrow, Del key, or the like to make the desired changes. You can insert new text by going to the spot desired and typing.

When you have modified the cell's contents correctly, press Enter.

## Erasing Cell Contents

Move the cell pointer to the cell.

| | |
|---|---|
| **Press:** | ⌨ **/** (to call up the menu) |
| **Select:** | **R**ange |
| **Select:** | **E**rase |

**If the range is correct, press** Enter

A range is a rectangular set of cells defined by the address of the upper-left cell, a period, and the lower-left cell. For example: A6.A6 or A6.B10.

## Inputting Repeating Characters

Position the cell pointer in the appropriate cell.

| | |
|---|---|
| **Type:** | ⌨ **\** |
| **Type:** | the character to be repeated |
| **Press:** | Enter |

You also can use

**@REPEAT(STRING,NUMBER)**

For example, @REPEAT("=",35) makes a line of 35 = signs.

## Changing Column Width

Position the cell pointer in any cell in the column you want to change the width of.

| | |
|---|---|
| **Press:** | ⌨ **/** (to call up the menu) |
| **Select:** | **W**orksheet |
| **Select:** | **C**olumn |
| **Select:** | **S**et-Width |

Type the new width or move the cursor left and right to change the width on the display screen.

**Press:**      Enter **(to complete the width change)**

## Moving Data

Move the cell pointer to the current location of the data.

**Press:**      /

**Select:**    **Move**

If the data to be moved is in more than one cell, move the cursor to highlight the entire range.

**Press:**      Enter

Move the cell pointer to the new location.

**Press:**      Enter

## Copying Data

Move the cell pointer to the current location of the data.

**Press:**      /

**Select:**    **Copy**

If the data to be copied is in more than one cell, move the cell pointer to highlight the entire range.

**Press:**      Enter

Move the cursor to the new location.

**Press:**      Enter

## Formatting Numbers

Formatting alters the way numbers are displayed in a cell. The most common formats are:

**Fixed format.**  Sets a fixed number of decimal places in all cells in the range.

**Currency format.** Adds a dollar sign and commas, if needed, and controls the number of decimal places displayed.

**Percent format.** Multiplies the number by 100, to move the decimal point two places right, and adds the percent sign.

If you typed 1234.565:

In Fixed format, two decimal places, the result would be 1234.57

In Fixed format, zero decimal places, the result would be 1235

In Currency format, two decimal places, the result would be $1,234.57

In Currency format, zero decimal places, the result would be $1,235.

To format the cell or cells:

| | |
|---|---|
| **Press:** | **[/] (to call up the menu)** |
| **Select:** | **Range** |
| **Select:** | **Format** |
| **Select:** | **the format desired** |
| **Type:** | **the desired number of decimal places** |
| **Type:** | **the range to format** |

## Inserting a Row or Column

Move the cell pointer to the spot where you want to insert data.

| | |
|---|---|
| **Press:** | **[/]** |
| **Select:** | **Worksheet** |
| **Select:** | **Insert** |
| **Select:** | **Row or Column** |

When Lotus 1-2-3 asks for the range, if you want more than one row or column, move the cell pointer to the desired number of rows or columns to be inserted.

**Press:**  Enter

## Reading a Disk File into Internal Memory

Make sure you have saved the worksheet currently on the screen. It will be erased when the new file is read.

**Press:**  /

**Select:**  **File**

**Select:**  **Retrieve**

Five file names appear, in alphabetic order, on the third line of the control panel.

**Press:**  F3  (to see all files saved on one screen)

**Move:**  the cell pointer to the desired file name

**Press:**  Enter

## Viewing the List of Files Saved on Disk

Just to view file names, not to retrieve files:

**Press:**  /

**Select:**  **File**

**Select:**  **List**

**Select:**  **Worksheet (to see only Lotus 1-2-3 spreadsheets), or**

**Select:**  **Other (to see all files saved on disk)**

**Press:**  Enter (to get back to the READY mode)

## Saving the Current Worksheet to Disk

**Press:**       /

**Select:**     **File**

**Select:**     **Save**

If the file has been saved previously, the file name appears on line 2 of the control panel. If you want to keep the same name, simply press Enter. Lotus 1-2-3 will then ask you if you want to Replace the file on disk with this one or Cancel the command (that is, not erase the file of the cited name that currently exists on disk).

If this is a new file or you want to change the name of file from what it was when you retrieved it from disk, simply type the file name and press Enter.

The mode indicator WAIT appears for a few seconds while the file is written to the disk.

## Erasing the On-Screen Worksheet and Starting Again

Make sure you have saved the worksheet if you want to get it back at a later time.

**Press:**       /

**Select:**     **Worksheet**

**Select:**     **Erase**

If the file hasn't been saved, Lotus 1-2-3 asks if you are sure you want to erase the current spreadsheet. If you don't want to save the current spreadsheet:

**Select:**     **Yes**

## Quitting Lotus 1-2-3 and Returning to DOS

Make sure the current worksheet has been saved if you want to use it later.

| | |
|---|---|
| **Press:** | / |
| **Select:** | **Quit** |
| **Select:** | **Yes** |
| **Select:** | **Exit** |

When the DOS prompt appears, you have exited Lotus 1-2-3.

## Printing the Worksheet

The file to be printed must be displayed on the screen. If it isn't, retrieve it.

Make sure the printer is turned on and ready.

Advance the paper to the top of a sheet if your printer is a dot-matrix printer.

Press (Home) to move the cell pointer to cell A1. This makes it easier to set the range.

Determine the upper-left corner cell and the lower-right corner cell in the print range.

| | |
|---|---|
| **Press:** | / |
| **Select:** | **Print** |
| **Select:** | **Printer** |
| **Select:** | **Range** |

Enter the range by either typing the address of the upper-left cell, a period, and the address of the lower-left cell or by anchoring the cursor and moving the cursor to the bottom of the range.

| | |
|---|---|
| **Press:** | (Enter) |

Select Align to reset the Lotus 1-2-3 line counter. (Since you have positioned the paper in the printer at the top of a sheet, Lotus 1-2-3 has to be told that it is starting at the top of a sheet.)

| Select: | **Go** |
|---------|--------|

Wait until the mode indicator is MENU again. Some printers have internal memory, called a buffer, in the printer. Buffers allow Lotus 1-2-3 to send a portion of the report at a time. This allows Lotus 1-2-3 to return to the MENU mode while the printer is still printing.

| Select: | **Page (to advance the paper to the top of the next sheet)** |
|---------|--------|

With some dot-matrix printers you will have to select Page twice to move the paper up far enough to tear it off. With a laser printer you *must* select Page to force the last page out of the printer.

| Select: | **Quit (to return to the READY mode)** |
|---------|--------|

## Sorting Data in the Worksheet

**Save the file to disk**

| Press: | ⌐/⌐ |
|--------|------|

| Select: | **Data** |
|---------|--------|

| Select: | **Sort** |
|---------|--------|

| Select: | **Data-Range** |
|---------|--------|

Make sure the data range includes the entire worksheet (all columns and rows), excluding headings and totals. The data range is the area to be rearranged when rows are moved. It must include all columns, not just the column being sorted. If you do this wrong, you can end up with one sorted column and data in other columns in the same position it was in before the sort.

**Enter the data range**

| Press: | ⌐Enter⌐ |
|--------|---------|

| Select: | **Primary-Key** |
|---------|--------|

Move the cursor to any cell in the column being sorted. The cell must exist inside the data range most recently selected. In other words, if the data range is defined as A5.G45 and you want to sort on column C, select any cell in column C from C5 to C45.

| | |
|---|---|
| **Press:** | Enter |
| **Type:** | A (for ascending) or D (for descending) |
| **Press:** | Enter |
| **Select:** | **Go** |

# Using Sample Documents and Spreadsheets

This section of the book contains sample worksheets that a small business person will find helpful. In several of the examples, the formulas are displayed using the Lotus 1-2-3 menu options Range, Format, and Text. This displays the formula in the cell instead of the answer. These are sample documents to guide you in developing your own personalized worksheets.

## Documents 1 and 2—Cash Flow Statement

Two versions of the same cash flow statements are presented. The first cash flow statement is displayed as it appears on the screen with normal formatting. The second version has the formulas revealed. It summarizes the increases and decreases of cash for the business.

## Document 3—Fixed Asset Record

This worksheet is used to retain important data about the company's assets. It includes data about the initial cost and data used to determine annual depreciation. Assets that have been discarded have information about the disposal.

## Document 4—Accounts Receivable Summary

This worksheet provides information about sales invoices. It is used to aid in managing customer charge accounts.

## Documents 5 and 6—Loan Amortization

This worksheet is used to determine how much of each payment is interest, annual interest paid on a loan, and the remaining principal after each payment. The first version shows how the worksheet appears with the data. The second version shows the worksheet with the formulas displayed.

## Document 7—Cash Register Daily Recap Sheet

This worksheet is used for the end of day cash register summary.

## Document 8—Check Reconciliation Form

This worksheet is used to prepare a reconciliation which compares the company checkbook balance to the balance indicated on the bank statement.

## Document 9—Balance Sheet

This worksheet shows the form used to list assets, liabilities, and owner's equity as of a specific date.

## Document 10—Income Statement

This worksheet lists the income and expense items in the proper format for a formal income statement.

## Document 1

| CASH FLOW | APR<br>Week 1 | APR<br>Week 2 | APR<br>Week 3 | APR<br>Week 4 |
|---|---|---|---|---|
| BEGINNING CASH | $3,000 | $4,850 | $200 | $950 |
| INCOME | | | | |
| COMMISSIONS | 4,000 | 4,000 | 4,000 | 4,000 |
| TOTAL REV. | 4,000 | 4,000 | 4,000 | 4,000 |
| EXPENDITURES | | | | |
| OWNER DRAW | 1,000 | 0 | 1,000 | 1,000 |
| INSURANCE | | | 800 | |
| RENT | 1,000 | 1,000 | 1,000 | 1,000 |
| SUPPLIES | | | 300 | |
| UTILITIES | 150 | 150 | 150 | 150 |
| LOAN PAYMENT | | 7,500 | | |
| TOTAL EXP. | 2,150 | 8,650 | 3,250 | 2,150 |
| ENDING CASH | $4,850 | $200 | $950 | $2,800 |

## Document 2

| | B          C | D | E | F |
|---|---|---|---|---|
| 2 | CASH FLOW | | APR | APR |
| 3 | | Week 1 | Week 2 | Week 3 |
| 4 | | | | |
| 5 | BEGINNING CASH | $3,000 | +D20 | +E20 |
| 6 | | | | |
| 7 | INCOME | | | |
| 8 | COMMISSIONS | 4000 | 4000 | 4000 |
| 9 | TOTAL REV. | +D8 | +E8 | +F8 |
| 10 | | | | |
| 11 | EXPENDITURES | | | |
| 12 | OWNER DRAW | 1000 | 0 | 1000 |
| 13 | INSURANCE | | | 800 |
| 14 | RENT | 1000 | 1000 | 1000 |
| 15 | SUPPLIES | | | 300 |
| 16 | UTILITIES | 150 | 150 | 150 |
| 17 | LOAN PAYMENT | | 7500 | |
| 18 | TOTAL EXP. | @SUM(D12..D17) | @SUM(E12..E17) | @SUM(F12..17) |
| 19 | | | | |
| 20 | ENDING CASH | +D5+D9−D18 | +E5+E9−E18 | +F5+F9−F18 |
| 21 | | | | |
| 22 | | | | |

## Document 3

XYZ COMPANY
FIXED ASSETS RECORD

| DATE ACQUIR. | DESCRIPTION | COST | EST. LIFE OF ASSET | ESTIMATED SCRAP/ TRADE VALUE | DATE SOLD | ACTUAL DISPOSAL VALUE |
|---|---|---|---|---|---|---|
| 10/18/91 | TI CALCULATOR | $70 | 5 | $0 | | |
| 10/18/91 | WIZ COMPUTER | $1,990 | 4 | $400 | 1/16/94 | $750 |
| 10/18/91 | WIZ PRINTER | $475 | 4 | $50 | 1/16/94 | $150 |
| 10/18/91 | OFFICE FURNITURE | $8,400 | 10 | $500 | | |
| 10/18/91 | DESK/CHAIR | $675 | 10 | $75 | | |
| 11/22/91 | AIR CONDITIONER | $2,600 | 6 | $500 | | |
| 10/18/92 | 92 CHRYSLER | $13,700 | 3 | $8,700 | | |
| 12/28/93 | PHONE SYSTEM | $1,800 | 5 | $400 | | |
| 3/12/94 | COPY MACHINE | $2,500 | 4 | $400 | | |
| 1/16/94 | WIZ ii COMPUTER | $2,200 | 3 | $700 | | |
| 1/16/94 | WOWEE PRINTER | $300 | 3 | $100 | | |

## Document 4

ACCOUNTS RECEIVABLE SUMMARY

| CUSTOMER NAME | INVOICE NUMBER | INVOICE DATE | INVOICE AMOUNT | PAID | DATE PAID |
|---|---|---|---|---|---|
| TOM JONES | 12222 | 09/03/93 | 400 | | |
| FRED SMITH | 13111 | 08/17/93 | 200 | Y | 09/21/93 |
| FRED SMITH | 13213 | 09/28/93 | 350 | Y | 10/25/93 |
| FRED SMITH | 14235 | 10/26/93 | 200 | | |
| FRED SMITH | 14325 | 11/01/93 | 400 | | |
| TOM JONES | 16354 | 10/29/93 | 300 | Y | 11/02/93 |
| TOM JONES | 17233 | 11/23/93 | 250 | | |

**Document 5**

LOAN AMORTIZATION

| | | |
|---|---|---|
| LOAN AMOUNT | $8,000.00 | |
| MONTHS | 24 | |
| INTEREST RATE | 7.5% | |
| MONTHLY PAYMENT | $360.00 | |
| LOAN DATE | MAR. 2, 1993 | |

| PAYMENT NUMBER | DATE | PAYMENT AMOUNT | INTEREST PORTION | PRINCIPAL PORTION | REMAINING PRINCIPAL BALANCE |
|---|---|---|---|---|---|
| | | | | | $8,000.00 |
| 1 | Mar-93 | $360.00 | $50.00 | $310.00 | $7,690.00 |
| 2 | Apr-93 | $360.00 | $48.06 | $311.94 | $7,378.06 |
| 3 | May-93 | $360.00 | $46.11 | $313.89 | $7,064.17 |
| 4 | Jun-93 | $360.00 | $44.15 | $315.85 | $6,748.32 |
| 5 | Jul-93 | $360.00 | $42.18 | $317.82 | $6,430.50 |
| 6 | Aug-93 | $360.00 | $40.19 | $319.81 | $6,110.69 |
| 7 | Sep-93 | $360.00 | $38.19 | $321.81 | $5,788.88 |
| 8 | Oct-93 | $360.00 | $36.18 | $323.82 | $5,465.06 |
| 9 | Nov-93 | $360.00 | $34.16 | $325.84 | $5,139.22 |
| 10 | Dec-93 | $360.00 | $32.12 | $327.88 | $4,811.34 |
| 11 | Jan-94 | $360.00 | $30.07 | $329.93 | $4,481.41 |
| 12 | Feb-94 | $360.00 | $28.01 | $331.99 | $4,149.42 |
| 13 | Mar-94 | $360.00 | $25.93 | $334.07 | $3,815.35 |
| 14 | Apr-94 | $360.00 | $23.85 | $336.15 | $3,479.20 |
| 15 | May-94 | $360.00 | $21.74 | $338.26 | $3,140.94 |
| 16 | Jun-94 | $360.00 | $19.63 | $340.37 | $2,800.57 |
| 17 | Jul-94 | $360.00 | $17.50 | $342.50 | $2,458.07 |
| 18 | Aug-94 | $360.00 | $15.36 | $344.64 | $2,113.43 |
| 19 | Sep-94 | $360.00 | $13.21 | $346.79 | $1,766.64 |
| 20 | Oct-94 | $360.00 | $11.04 | $348.96 | $1,417.68 |
| 21 | Nov-94 | $360.00 | $8.86 | $351.14 | $1,066.54 |
| 22 | Dec-94 | $360.00 | $6.67 | $353.33 | $713.21 |
| 23 | Jan-95 | $360.00 | $4.46 | $355.54 | $357.67 |
| 24 | Feb-95 | $359.91 | $2.24 | $357.67 | $0.00 |
| | TOTALS | $8,639.91 | $639.91 | $8,000.00 | |

# Using Sample Documents and Spreadsheets

## Document 6

| B | C | D | E | F | G | H | I | J |
|---|---|---|---|---|---|---|---|---|
| LOAN AMORTIZATION | | | | | | | | |
| LOAN AMOUNT | | | | $8,000 | | | | |
| MONTHS | | | | 24 | | | | |
| INTEREST RATE | | | | 7.5% | | | | |
| MONTHLY PAYMENT | | | | @PMT(D4,D6/12,D5) | | | | |
| LOAN DATE | | | | MAR. 2, 1993 | | | | |
| | | | | | | | | REMAINING |
| PAYMENT | | PAYMENT | | INTEREST | | PRINCIPAL | | PRINCIPAL |
| NUMBER | DATE | AMOUNT | | PORTION | | PORTION | | BALANCE |
| | | | | | | | | $8,000 |
| 1 | Mar-93 | +$D$7 | | +J12*($D$6/12) | | +D13-F13 | | +J12-H13 |
| 2 | Apr-93 | +$D$7 | | +J13*($D$6/12) | | +D14-F14 | | +J13-H14 |
| 3 | May-93 | +$D$7 | | +J14*($D$6/12) | | +D15-F15 | | +J14-H15 |
| 4 | Jun-93 | +$D$7 | | +J15*($D$6/12) | | +D16-F16 | | +J15-H16 |
| 5 | Jul-93 | +$D$7 | | +J16*($D$6/12) | | +D17-F17 | | +J16-H17 |
| 6 | Aug-93 | +$D$7 | | +J17*($D$6/12) | | +D18-F18 | | +J17-H18 |
| 7 | Sep-93 | +$D$7 | | +J18*($D$6/12) | | +D19-F19 | | +J18-H19 |
| 8 | Oct-93 | +$D$7 | | +J19*($D$6/12) | | +D20-F20 | | +J19-H20 |
| 9 | Nov-93 | +$D$7 | | +J20*($D$6/12) | | +D21-F21 | | +J20-H21 |
| 10 | Dec-93 | +$D$7 | | +J21*($D$6/12) | | +D22-F22 | | +J21-H22 |
| 11 | Jan-94 | +$D$7 | | +J22*($D$6/12) | | +D23-F23 | | +J22-H23 |
| 12 | Feb-94 | +$D$7 | | +J23*($D$6/12) | | +D24-F24 | | +J23-H24 |
| 13 | Mar-94 | +$D$7 | | +J24*($D$6/12) | | +D25-F25 | | +J24-H25 |
| 14 | Apr-94 | +$D$7 | | +J25*($D$6/12) | | +D26-F26 | | +J25-H26 |
| 15 | May-94 | +$D$7 | | +J26*($D$6/12) | | +D27-F27 | | +J26-H27 |
| 16 | Jun-94 | +$D$7 | | +J27*($D$6/12) | | +D28-F28 | | +J27-H28 |
| 17 | Jul-94 | +$D$7 | | +J28*($D$6/12) | | +D29-F29 | | +J28-H29 |
| 18 | Aug-94 | +$D$7 | | +J29*($D$6/12) | | +D30-F30 | | +J29-H30 |
| 19 | Sep-94 | +$D$7 | | +J30*($D$6/12) | | +D31-F31 | | +J30-H31 |
| 20 | Oct-94 | +$D$7 | | +J31*($D$6/12) | | +D32-F32 | | +J31-H32 |
| 21 | Nov-94 | +$D$7 | | +J32*($D$6/12) | | +D33-F33 | | +J32-H33 |
| 22 | Dec-94 | +$D$7 | | +J33*($D$6/12) | | +D34-F34 | | +J33-H34 |
| 23 | Jan-95 | +$D$7 | | +J34*($D$6/12) | | +D35-F35 | | +J34-H35 |
| 24 | Feb-95 | +J35 | | +J35*($D$6/12) | | +D36-F36 | | 0 |
| | TOTALS | $8,639.91 | | $639.91 | | $8,000.00 | | |

TO GET THE COLUMN OF DATES, USE THE / DATA FILL MENU.
SET THE RANGE TO INCLUDE 24 CELLS IN THE DESIRED COLUMN.
USE @datevalue("03/02/93") AS THE START, 31 AS THE STEP,
AND 99999 AS THE STOP VALUE.
THEN FORMAT THE COLUMN WITH / RANGE FORMAT DATE 3 (mmm-yy)

INTEREST IS REMAINING PRINCIPAL FROM PREVIOUS MONTH TIMES THE
INTEREST RATE DIVIDED BY 12 (for the monthly rate).

IN ORDER TO HAVE TOTALS COME OUT CORRECT, IT WAS NECESSARY TO
USE THE @ROUND FUNCTION. @round(FORMULA,NO OF DEC PLACES)

ex: cell F13: @ROUND(+J12*($D$6/12),2)

**Document 7**

DATE: _____ DAILY CASH SHEET

BEGINNING FUND IN REGISTER _____

ADD

      TAXABLE SALES _____

      NONTAXABLE SALES _____

      SALES TAX COLLECTED _____

      CASH REC'D ON ACCOUNT _____

SUBTOTAL _____

DEDUCT

      PAID OUTS _____

      SALES ON ACCOUNT _____

               TOTAL DEDUCTIONS _____

AMOUNT OF CASH THAT SHOULD BE IN THE REGISTER _____

_____

ACTUAL CASH IN REGISTER

      CHECKS _____

      $20 BILLS _____

      $10 BILLS _____

      $5 BILLS

                  _____

      $1 BILLS

      QUARTERS _____

      DIMES _____

      NICKELS _____

      PENNIES _____

      OTHER _____

ACTUAL CASH IN THE CASH REGISTER _____

CASH OVER (CASH SHORT) ===============

**107**

**Document 8**

BANK RECONCILIATION FOR THE PERIOD ENDING:

BANK STATEMENT BALANCE:                                                     $_____

ADD DEPOSIT(S) IN TRANSIT

_____ $_____          _____ $_____

_____ $_____          _____ $_____

                         TOTAL ADDITIONS          $_____

LESS OUTSTANDING CHECKS

_____ $_____          _____ $_____

_____ $_____          _____ $_____

_____ $_____          _____ $_____

_____ $_____          _____ $_____

_____ $_____          _____ $_____

_____ $_____          _____ $_____

_____ $_____          _____ $_____

                         TOTAL DEDUCTIONS          $_____

               ADJUSTED BANK STATEMENT BALANCE          $_____

_____

CHECKBOOK BALANCE:                                                     $_____

ADD

       INTEREST EARNED          $_____

       _____ $_____

                         TOTAL ADDITIONS          $_____

LESS

       SERVICE CHARGE(S)          $_____

       _____ $_____

                         TOTAL DEDUCTIONS          $_____

       ADJUSTED CHECKBOOK BALANCE          $_____

**Document 9**

```
                          XYZ COMPANY
                          BALANCE SHEET
                          DEC 31, 19___

CURRENT ASSETS                    CURRENT LIABILITIES

    CASH                 x,xxx         NOTES PAYABLE        x,xxx

    SECURITIES           x,xxx         ACCOUNTS PAYABLE     x,xxx

    ACCOUNTS RECEIVABLE  x,xxx         ACCRUED EXPENSES     x,xxx

    PREPAID EXPENSES     x,xxx         ACCRUED TAXES        x,xxx

    TOTAL CURRENT ASSETS x,xxx         TOTAL CURRENT LIAB.  x,xxx

PROPERTY AND EQUIPMENT            LONG TERM DEBT

    LAND                 x,xxx         MORTGAGE PAYABLE     x,xxx

    BUILDING             x,xxx         AUTO LOAN PAYABLE    x,xxx

    EQUIPMENT            x,xxx         TOTAL LONG TERM DEBT x,xxx

    DEPRECIATION        (x,xxx)    OWNERS EQUITY

    TOTAL FIXED ASSETS   x,xxx         J. DOE, CAPITAL      x,xxx

TOTAL ASSETS             x,xxx     TOTAL LIAB. AND EQUITY   x,xxx
```

**Document 10**

XYZ CONSULTING
INCOME STATEMENT
YEAR ENDING DEC 31, 1994

|  | 1994 | 1993 |
|---|---|---|
| REVENUE |  |  |
| SALES | XX,XXX | XX,XXX |
| LESS SALES RETURNS | XX,XXX | XX,XXX |
| NET SALES | XX,XXX | XX,XXX |
| COST OF GOODS SOLD |  |  |
| BEGINNING INVENTORY | XX,XXX | XX,XXX |
| PLUS PURCHASES | XX,XXX | XX,XXX |
| GOODS AVAILABLE FOR SALE | XX,XXX | XX,XXX |
| LESS ENDING INVENTORY | XX,XXX | XX,XXX |
| COST OF GOODS SOLD | XX,XXX | XX,XXX |
| GROSS PROFIT | XX,XXX | XX,XXX |
| OPERATING EXPENSES | XX,XXX | XX,XXX |
| NET PROFIT FROM OPERATIONS | XX,XXX | XX,XXX |
| NON-OPERATING EXPENSES |  |  |
| INTEREST EXPENSE | XX,XXX | XX,XXX |
| NET INCOME | XX,XXX | XX,XXX |

APPENDIX

# Glossary of Key Terms

**@NOW function**   The function that tells Lotus 1-2-3 to enter the current date any time the worksheet is retrieved from disk.

**@PMT**   The function used to calculate monthly payment on a loan. The @PMT function is written: @PMT(LOAN AMOUNT, INTEREST RATE,NUMBER OF PAYMENTS)

**@SUM**   The function that tells Lotus 1-2-3 to calculate the sum of the value in the cells cited in the function.

**A data**   The worksheet data that determines the size of each "slice" in a pie chart or each bar in a bar graph.

**Absolute address**   A cell address that cannot be changed if the formula in which it appears is copied. To make a cell address absolute, precede each element in it with a dollar sign. For example: $F$20. *See also* Relative address.

**Anchoring**   Signaling Lotus 1-2-3, by entering a period, that you have finished typing the beginning address of the cells that define the target range. Anchoring enables pointing.

**Arithmetic operator**   A symbol that tell Lotus 1-2-3 what math operations to do with data in a formula. The arithmetic operators are + (for addition), – (for subtraction), * (for multiplication), and / (for division).

**Ascending order**   An arrangement in which items are in sequence from lowest to highest.

**Asset**   An item of value owned by a business. *See also* Current asset, Fixed Asset.

**Automatic fill feature**   A feature that allows you to indicate a range to fill, the start value and the increment. Lotus 1-2-3 will automatically enter the data for you.

**Balance sheet**   A document that lists the value of assets, liabilities, and owner's equity as of a specific date.

**Cash flow statement**   A document that provides a summary of cash receipts and cash payments of a business for a period of time, such as a month or year. It reports on the impact of a company's operating, investing, and financing activities on the cash flow for an accounting period.

**Cell**   In a worksheet, the area where a row and column intersect.

**Cell pointer**   A rectangle that contrasts with the background color of your screen. The cell pointer allows you to access different cells of a worksheet.

**Control panel**   The top three rows of the Lotus 1-2-3 screen. Displays information such as current cell address, format, column width, cell contents, and mode indicator. Additionally, the control panel will display data as you are typing it, and the menu.

**Current asset**   Cash or an item of value that will convert into cash during one year or be used up in one year.

**Current liability**   A liability that must be paid within the year. *See also* Long-term liability.

**Data range**   All the cells to be moved when sorting.

**Default**   The value assumed. In Lotus 1-2-3, you can set a default in regard to disk drive, default column width, and label prefix, for example.

**Depreciation**   The decline in value over time, due to obsolescence or physical deterioration.

**Descending order**   An arrangement in which items are in sequence from highest to lowest.

**Equity**   The ownership rights to the assets.

**Expense**   The cost of doing business. Expenses include rent, wages, telephone, insurance, depreciation, and advertising.

**Explode**   To have a "slice" of a pie chart stick out from the pie to draw emphasis to the data the slice represents.

**External memory**   Relatively permanent storage for data; usually, a disk.

**Fixed asset**   An item of value of "permanent" nature, usually with a life of over one year.

**Footer**   A single line printed at the bottom of all pages.

**Format**   The manner in which numbers are displayed.

**Formula**   An instruction that tells Lotus 1-2-3 to calculate the contents of a cell by using data from other cells. The expression +D5+D6-D7/D8*D9 is a formula.

**Function**   A predefined formula, such as SUM or AVERAGE. You provide the parameters in the formula. For example: @SUM(A4.A10).

**Function keys**   Allow you to implement, in one keystroke, instructions that take the computer several steps to complete. In this sense, the function keys represent shortcuts.

**Gross profit**   The total profit before expenses. *See also* Net profit.

**Hardware**   The equipment that forms the computer system.

**Header**   A single line printed at the top of all pages.

**Income statement**   A document that lists the revenue and expenses over a period of time. Basically, it answers the question "How much money is the business making?"

**Internal memory**   A portion of the computer that stores the data and program currently being worked on. Programs must be brought into internal memory before they can be run; data must reside in internal memory before it can be processed. Also called random access memory, or RAM.

**Label**   Alphabetic data, such as column headings, or numeric data that is not used in math calculations.

**Label prefix**   A code that precedes label data; determines how alphabetic data will be displayed. The code ' determines that text will be left-justified, " right-justifies the text, and ^ centers the text.

**Legend**   A graph label that identifies which column of data in the worksheet a bar represents.

**Liability**   Money owed.

**Long-term liability**   A liability that won't be paid within the year. *See also* Current liability.

**Microprocessor**   The component that performs the bulk of data processing in a computer. It analyzes instructions and directs other parts of the computer to execute the instructions. The 8088, 80286, 80386, 80486, and Pentium are examples of microprocessors used in IBM and IBM-compatible microcomputers.

**Net income**   Total income minus total expenses. Also called net profit.

**Nonoperating expenses**   An expense such as interest on a mortgage and a fine or penalty not incurred in the normal course of business. *See also* Operating expenses.

**Nonoperating income**   Income derived from sources other than normal business functions. *See also* Operating income.

**Operating expense**   An expense incurred during the normal operation of a business. *See also* Nonoperating expense.

**Operating income**   Income derived solely from the operation of a business. *See also* Nonoperating income.

**Owner's equity**   Assets minus liabilities.

**Pointing**   Using the cell pointer to highlight the range instead of typing the range.

**Random-access memory (RAM)**   See Internal memory.

**Range**   In a spreadsheet, a block of cells, defined in a formula by typing the address of the upper-left cell, a period, and the address of the lower-right cell. For example: A4:G7.

**Relative address**   An address, in a formula, that changes according to the new location of the formula. *See also* Absolute address.

**Repeat code**   The message Lotus 1-2-3 receives when you press the backslash, \. The message tells Lotus 1-2-3 to repeat, in the cell, any character typed after \.

**Revenue**   The money a company earned in the process of doing business.

**Software**   Computer programs; the instructions that tell the hardware what to do.

**Sort key**   The field by which you are sorting.

**Start value**   The starting number in a series of numbers being entered with the Data, Fill command.

**Status line**   At the bottom of the Lotus 1-2-3 screen, the area that contains information about the date, time, and various settings (such as the setting of Caps Lock and Num Lock).

**Stop value**   The number that stops the Data Fill series. Lotus 1-2-3 will stop the fill when either the range of cells is filled or the number generated equals the stop value. Lotus 1-2-3 defaults the stop value at 8191. The user can either accept this value or type his or her own stop value.

**Window**   The portion of the worksheet that is visible on the screen.

**Working capital**   The assets that can be applied to the operation of the business.

**Worksheet**   A grid of rows and colums, in which you store data and formulas.

**X data**   The worksheet data that will be used to label each "slice" in a pie chart or to label the bars in a bar graph.

# Notes

# Index

# About the Author

Bill Barth has taught Accounting and Computer Science at the college level for over 25 years. Presently he is a professor in the Business Division at Cayuga Community College in Auburn, New York. He teaches courses in Introductory Accounting, COBOL programming, RPG programming, DOS, Windows, Lotus 1-2-3, Excel, WordPerfect, dBASE, and Microsoft Works. Additionally, he has taught microcomputer software seminars in business and industry for the past 10 years.

In 1989 Cayuga Community College presented Professor Barth the Excellence In Teaching Award. This award is presented annually to professors selected by the administration of the college.